MUAY THAI

MUAY THAI

Kru Tony Moore

First published in 2004 by
New Holland Publishers Ltd
London • Cape Town • Sydney • Auckland
www.newhollandpublishers.com

86 Edgware Road
London W2 2EA
United Kingdom

80 McKenzie Street
Cape Town 8001
South Africa

14 Aquatic Drive
Frenchs Forest, NSW 2086
Australia

218 Lake Road
Northcote, Auckland
New Zealand

ISBN 1 84330 596 8 (paperback)
ISBN 1 84330 751 0 (hardback)

PUBLISHER: Mariëlle Renssen
PUBLISHING MANAGERS: Claudia Dos Santos, Simon Pooley
COMMISSIONING EDITOR: Alfred LeMaitre
STUDIO MANAGER : Richard MacArthur
EDITOR: Katja Splettstoesser
DESIGNER: Elmari Kuyler
ILLUSTRATOR: Elmari Kuyler
PICTURE RESEARCHER: Karla Kik
PRODUCTION: Myrna Collins
CONSULTANT: Tim Mousel

Reproduction by Hirt & Carter (Cape) Pty Ltd
Printed and bound in Malaysia by Times Offset (M) Sdn. Bhd.
2 4 6 8 10 9 7 5 3 1

DEDICATION

For my brother David Moore (1947–2002) who tragically
passed away; you are missed by all your family and friends

DISCLAIMER

The author and publishers have made every effort to ensur
that the information contained in this book was accurate at th
time of going to press, and accept no responsibility for ar
injury or inconvenience sustained by any person using th
book or following the advice provided herein.

AUTHOR'S ACKNOWLEDGMENTS

I would like to extend special thanks to my wife Karen, without whose tolerance, understanding and encouragement this book would not have been possible; my children and students Sandra and Steven; Khun Virasak Tokakuna for opening doors for me in Thailand; the late Arjarn Nai Samai Messamarn, my teacher: I will try my utmost to live up to your ideals, you are greatly missed; Mae Kru Messamarn and my brothers Arjarn Werayut and Arjarn Sira; Arjarn Panya Kraitus for his support and tuition; Arjarn Yodthong; the late Mr Bunyuen Suvanatadha and Mr Sanit Khonark (I.F.M.A.); Pramaha Pratum, head monk at Wat Phraya Tham. Thanks also to Khun Apidej Sithirun; Arjarn Lec Chaikeawrung, Master Boonckun, Arjarn Tooey Yodthong, Samart and Kongtoranee Payakarun, Kaosai Galaxy, Khun Dermsak, Kru Taworn, Kru Reungnimit, Ronachai Soonkilanongki, Khun Thakoon, Arjarn Chorp; the Songchai family; Master Sken; my brothers, Steve Wilson and Clint Heyliger; Mrs Mudita Karnasuta; and finally all my Muay Thai friends: together we have proven that Muay Thai is the king of all martial arts.

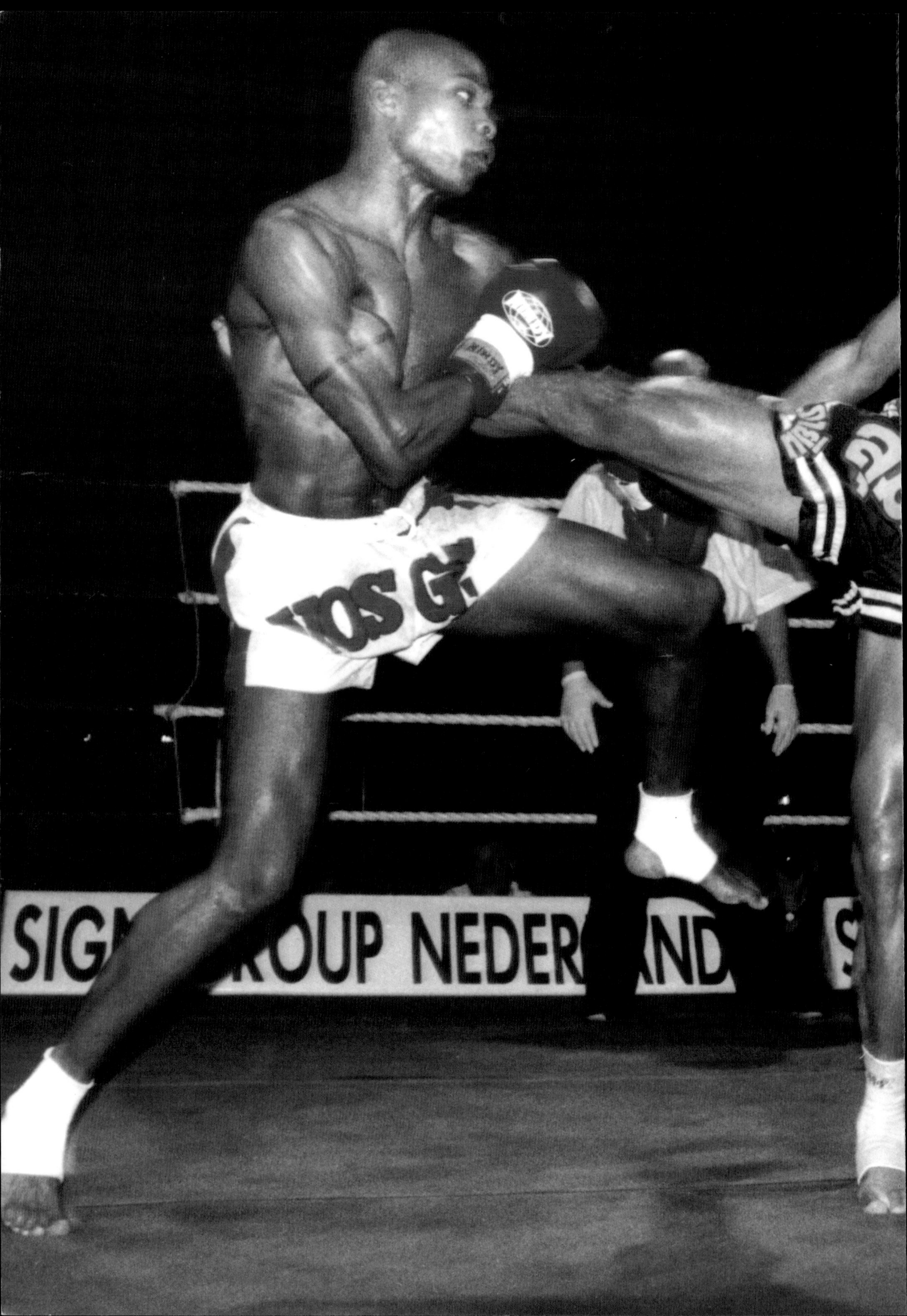
SIGM ROUP NEDER AND
VOS G

CONTENTS

INTRODUCTION

Muay Thai — Thai Boxing — can trace its origins back more than 2000 years to the tribes of the Ao Lai who migrated from southern China down to the central plains of Siam, known today as Thailand. It is difficult to prove conclusively when and where the art originated, because all records of Thai history were destroyed in the Ayuddhaya period when Burmese invaders sacked the ancient capital. Thus, the history of Muay Thai has been pieced together from remnants of information that escaped this destruction, and that were passed down the generations by word of mouth from teacher to student.

above A STATUETTE OF KING NARESUAN THE GREAT, WHOSE SHRINE IS LOCATED AT WAT YAI CHAI MONGKOL IN AYUDDHAYA. MANY THAI BOXERS MAKE A PILGRIMAGE TO THE SHRINE BEFORE BOUTS.

opposite THAIS ARE VERY PROUD OF THEIR TRADITIONAL MARTIAL ART, SO MUCH SO THAT BOXERS BEGIN TRAINING AT A VERY EARLY AGE.

Inspirational figures

Before ascending the throne of Siam in 1590, King Naresuan the Great, who reigned in the Ayuddhaya period, had been known popularly as the Black Prince. A hostage of Burma until the age of 16, he was renowned for his bravery even prior to freeing Siam from the chains of Burmese slavery. In 1584 he returned to Siam renouncing allegiance to Burma on behalf of his father King Maha Tammaraja.

The King of Burma took great exception to losing his Siamese provinces and sent an increasing number of soldiers to fight against the Siamese. The armies of Siam, under King Naresuan, defeated the Burmese in successive battles. Finally an army of approximately 250,000 men was despatched from Burma to try to subdue Siam once and for all. History tells many tales of King Naresuan's courage but perhaps the greatest feat of all was what happened in this final battle.

King Naresuan faced overwhelming odds as the Burmese army far outnumbered the Siamese forces. This great warrior mounted an armoured war elephant and charged through his army to the frontline. Seeing the Crown Prince of Burma also seated on a war elephant, King Naresuan challenged the Prince to single combat. After a fierce skirmish the king cut the Crown Prince in half from shoulder to hip. The Burmese army, seeing their leader slain, turned and fled back to Burma. Through this singular act of bravery, King Naresuan freed Siam forever.

King Taksin the Great
King Taksin the Great ruled from 1767 to 1782. He rose to fame, like the legendary phoenix, from the ashes of Ayuddhaya, the then capital of Siam. The Burmese invaders had plundered and looted the city, vandalizing and destroying all of Siam's historical records in 1767. After a great battle in which the Burmese took Ayuddhaya, King Taksin, with 500

followers, managed to escape, travelling east to Rayong. Here he began to build a new army with the renowned warrior Phraya Pichai Daab Hak as his commander in chief. *Daab hak* means 'broken sword'; this nickname was earned when, during one of the many fierce battles, one of Phraya Pichai's swords was broken in two. The brave general continued to fight on, ultimately leading King Taksin's army to yet another glorious victory.

With his small army King Taksin declared war on Burma. Using guerrilla tactics the army attacked Burma in small bands, continuously harrying the enemy and totally destroying their supply routes. As word of his exploits spread, so inspired were the Siamese people

A MINIATURE STATUE OF KING TAKSIN (BACK). THE ACTUAL MONUMENT OF THE KING IS LOCATED AT WONG WIAN YAI ROUNDABOUT IN BANGKOK AND DEPICTS HIM ON HORSEBACK CARRYING A SWORD. THE STATUETTE OF PHRAYA PICHAI DAAB HAK (FRONT) IS A REPLICA OF THE STATUE LOCATED IN UTTARADIT IN NORTHERN THAILAND.

that many more rallied to his cause. Eventually the army was large enough to make an all-out counterattack on Ayuddhaya which was still under Burmese control. Although still outnumbered two to one, he attacked and routed the Burmese with great losses amid the enemy ranks. This was only the beginning, for throughout his reign the country was constantly at war.

King Taksin many times distinguished himself in battle. A bold and courageous military strategist, he decided to move the Siamese capital to Thonburi because the new site was easier to defend than Ayuddhaya, which now lay in uninhabitable ruins. In battle King Taksin's strategy and fighting spirit were unsurpassed. After many hard-fought battles he managed to reunite the kingdom.

Pra Chao Suua

The Tiger King, Pra Chao Suua (1662—1709), loved all sports but especially Muay Thai. He was famous for disguising himself as a peasant and travelling around the country participating very successfully in Muay Thai bouts at public festivals. At one such festival he fought two champions, defeating both, and was paid two *ticals* by the ringmaster. He then left undetected, nobody having been aware of the royal presence in their midst. At another village he came up against a fighter known as Panthainorasingh. The bout was very well matched with neither boxer gaining the upper hand. The bout ended when tax collectors arriving at the village interrupted it. Worried that his identity might be revealed, the king had to escape quickly. However, so impressed was he with Panthainorasin's fighting skill that he asked the talented pugilist to come to work for him as the steersman of his royal barge (today's equivalent of a personal bodyguard who drives the getaway car!).

Nai Khanom Tom

Probably the most famous Muay Thai boxer of all time was Nai Khanom Tom, known as the Father of Muay Thai. He was the first ever Muay Thai boxer to fight in another country. In 1774 the Burmese monarch, King

THE GREAT WARRIOR KING TAKSIN DEPICTED ON HORSEBACK IN THE HEAT OF BATTLE.

and were influential in shaping it into the art it is today. The bravery of King Naresuan, the tactics of King Taksin, and Pra Chao Suua's love of Muay Thai are integral to the warrior spirit that lies at the heart of this fascinating martial art.

Origins and development

King Naresuan the Great and King Taksin are reputed to have studied at the Wat Phutthai Sawan (Buddhai Swan) in Ayuddhaya. This temple is believed to have been built by the first king of Ayuddhaya, Pra Chao U-Thong, known as King Rama Thibodi, around 1350. It was the site of a school for martial arts for many centuries. The original teachers were Buddhist monks who taught fighting with the sword. Nobody is certain where these monks came from but it is possible that they came from Lanna, the northern kingdom.

ONE OF THE MANY RUINED TEMPLES WITHIN THE OLD CITY WALLS OF AYUDDHAYA WHICH CAN STILL BE SEEN TODAY. MUAY THAI WAS AT ITS ZENITH DURING THE AYUDDHAYA PERIOD.

The Phutthai Sawan School taught the art of Krabi Krabong (Thai weapons art). There is some debate among scholars whether Muay Thai evolved from Krabi Krabong or developed separately alongside it. Some scholars argue that when the Thais were constantly fighting for survival, besides using weapons such as swords, spears, pikes and bows and arrows, they also used hand-to-hand combat skills using the body's natural weapons, namely their hands and feet, and knees and elbows.

Mangra, captured him during battle with Siamese forces. Nai Khanom Tom's prowess as a boxer was to save his life and win him his freedom. Challenged to fight against 10 of Burma's best Bando boxers, he defeated them all and was granted his freedom. Annually 17 March is a very special date in the Muay Thai calendar, being *Nai Khanom Tom Night,* when a special event is promoted to commemorate this exceptional Muay Thai boxer.

King Naresuan the Great, King Taksin and the Tiger King, Pra Chao Suua, were all exponents of Muay Thai

The original name for Muay Thai was Mai See Sawk. Later names for the art included Muay Pahuyuth; in southern Thailand it was known as Chaiya Boxing: Muay Tai during the mid-Ratanakosin period; and also as Siamese Boxing. All of these arts can be categorized as Muay Kaad-cheurk, meaning 'fighting with bound fists, or Muay Boran, meaning 'old or antique boxing'. Many of the techniques from ancient times have been lost, although Muay Pahuyuth is still taught in its original form. From earliest times the knowledge of Muay Pahuyuth has been passed down from teacher to teacher, the last known grand master being Arjarn Ket Sriyapai whose student, Arjarn Panya Kraitus, still teaches Muay Pahuyuth today.

During ancient times, fights could be a dangerous affair. Bouts were fought with hemp-bound hands dipped in either resin or starch. This hardened the hemp, making the hands lethal weapons. It is also suggested in some history records that, in extreme bouts, the hemp rope was sprinkled with finely ground glass or sand. These bouts were said to have been fought until first blood was drawn or even to the death! It wasn't until the reign of King Rama VII around 1929 when the use of boxing gloves was introduced, making the sport a lot less hazardous for the participants.

Over the centuries Muay Thai's popularity grew to such an extent that on 1 March 1941 the Office of the Crown Property laid the foundation stone for Rajadamnern Stadium in Bangkok. World War II intervened and halted its construction but the project resumed once more in August 1945. A committee was formed to oversee the many rules and regulations of the martial art as well as the conduct of bouts, and on 23 December, just four short months after the stadium opened for its very first match, the modern sport of Muay Thai was born.

In the past Muay Thai has also been known as:

- Mai See Sawk
- Muay Pahuyuth
- Chaiya Boxing
- Muay Tai
- Siamese Boxing

They can be categorized as Muay Kaad-cheurk, meaning 'fighting with bound fists' or Muay Boran, meaning 'old or antique boxing'.

The spread of Muay Thai worldwide

The opening of the Rajadamnern Stadium was soon to bring Muay Thai to prominence outside of Thailand. In 1950, an American businessman sponsored two Thai boxers from Thailand to give a demonstration of Muay Thai in Rochester, New York. In 1962 yet another

MANY SCHOLARS AGREE THAT MUAY THAI HAS ITS ORIGINS IN KRABI KRABONG, THE WEAPONS ART OF THAILAND.

YOUNG BOXERS PRACTISING MUAY THAI OUTDOORS IN THE GROUNDS OF THE PHRAYA PICHAI MONUMENT IN UTTARADIT, NORTHERN THAILAND.

American businessman sponsored a group of Thai boxers, who gave a demonstration of Muay Thai at the Seattle World Fair.

In the early 1970s there were frequent visits to Thailand by Japanese martial artists quick to realize that martial arts could become a very popular spectators' sport. Omitting the knee and elbow strikes that were not part of the Japanese arts of karate, judo and jiu jitsu, and opting to wear long trousers instead of Muay Thai shorts, they initiated the development of the sport of kickboxing.

It was Mr Osamu Noguchi who is credited with the founding and promotion of the sport of kickboxing. Mr Noguchi opened his own kickboxing gym-cum-coffee shop in the centre of Bangkok which appealed to the local fight pundits. Unfortunately he erred by claiming that kickboxing was superior to the mother art of Muay Thai. Following what was considered by the Thais to be an outrageous claim, his reign in Thai society was short-lived and he quickly retreated home to Tokyo.

Derivatives of Muay Thai

There was even further corruption of the rules of Muay Thai when kickboxing spread to the USA. There the use of low kicks was outlawed and fighters were expected to wear protective gear such as shin guards and foot boots. These American modifications included renaming the sport 'full-contact karate'. Today full-contact karate and kickboxing exist as separate entities, although with the myriad variations of their rules, these sports are still very much in their infancy.

Thai boxing in Europe

During the mid-1970s, Muay Thai spread to Europe. The Europeans, contrary to the Americans, kept the name Muay Thai, translated as Thai Boxing, along with all the traditions, rituals, rules and regulations.

In January 1984 the World Muay Thai Association was founded in Amsterdam. Countries represented at the meeting to formalize this were Thailand, Netherlands, England, France, Italy, Norway, Sweden and Spain. Dutch representative, Mr Thom Harinck, later founded the European Muay Thai Association. Both these associations were very successful in promoting the art of Muay Thai throughout Europe and, for the first time, foreign boxers were allowed to compete in Thailand. Success followed success and soon it was not unusual to see Muay Thai fighters from all over the world training at boxing camps in Thailand and fighting in the renowned Rajadamnern and Lumpini stadiums in Bangkok. Further developments in the martial art were soon to follow.

In 1986 Mr Bunyuen Suvanatadha founded the Amateur Muay Thai Association of Thailand (AMTAT). A few months later, the association expanded its interests to cover Southeast Asia and then internationally with the formation of the International Federation of Muay Thai Amateurs (IFMA). The amateur system of Muay Thai requires boxers to wear body shields and head guards. This safety precaution encouraged many more people worldwide to take up the art because it made the sport very much safer for participants.

Although the association had, for a number of years, organized the Prince's Cup competition for Thai competitors, it was decided in 1994 to organize an international event, the King's Cup. By the second King's Cup event in 1997, there were no less than 25 nations taking part in the competition.

The first European Amateur Muay Thai championship was held in Manchester, England, in 1997 and was organized by the British Thai Boxing Council with eight European nations taking part. The vice president of the International Federation of Muay Thai Amateurs, Mr Bunyuen Suvanatadha, was a very proud witness of the first, successful, amateur Muay Thai event held outside of Thailand.

Today, professional and amateur Muay Thai associations co-exist in nearly every country throughout the world and many world governments have now accepted Muay Thai as a sport. Of even greater importance is that Muay Thai has taken its rightful position as one of the world's most respected martial arts, as is evident by the now recognized saying: 'Muay Thai, Moradok Thai, Moradok Loke', that is, Thai boxing, Thai heritage, world heritage.

STARTING OUT

Muay Thai – A Beginner's Guide

Most people wanting to take up Muay Thai will usually do so on a recommendation from a friend or family member who already trains at a school or camp. However, it is vital when looking to join a Muay Thai class to find a reputable club registered with an official governing body. The instructor should have relevant certificates and qualifications from that governing body and these should be prominently displayed or readily available to a new student for inspection.

When you have found a prospective club, its instructors should be open to you viewing the facilities. The instructor will more than likely invite you to watch a class. A well-organized school or training camp should have a safety policy, public liability insurance, professional indemnity cover for the instructor and personal accident insurance for its students. The latter should provide cover for full-contact competition. You should always remember that Muay Thai is a full-contact martial art. The vast majority of people who enrol at a Muay Thai school do so to keep fit or for self-defence reasons. Few students actually wish to participate in competitions. This would not apply in Bangkok, however, where all boxers join a school to enter into the sport professionally.

Although you may only wish to practise Muay Thai as a means of self-defence, the martial art's exercises such as skipping, shadow boxing, and pad- and bag work will enable you to reap inestimable benefits in terms of both physical and mental fitness.

Sparring is an essential part of learning Muay Thai. For this purpose, most schools and training camps will provide safety equipment such as shin guards, head guards and approximately 14oz boxing gloves, with the students providing their own equipment in terms of a mouthpiece and groin protector. Light and controlled sparring is undertaken to practise attack and defence techniques.

above STUDENTS OF MUAY THAI ARE TAUGHT THE PRINCIPLES OF HARD WORK, SELF-DISCIPLINE AND PERSEVERANCE FROM AN EARLY AGE.

opposite IT IS BETTER TO WEAR LARGE SIZE BOXING GLOVES DURING FREE SPARRING; 14, 16 OR EVEN 18oz ARE PREFERABLE AS THE LARGER THE GLOVES' SURFACE AREA, THE LESS CHANCE THERE IS OF CAUSING INJURY TO YOUR PARTNER.

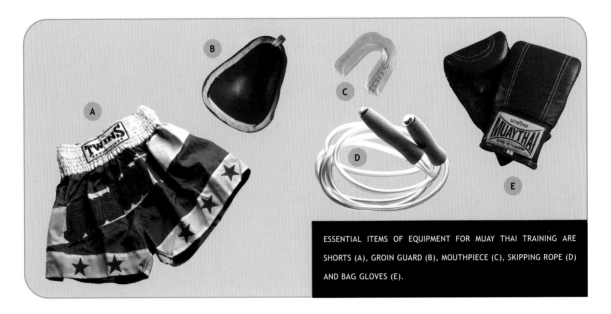

ESSENTIAL ITEMS OF EQUIPMENT FOR MUAY THAI TRAINING ARE SHORTS (A), GROIN GUARD (B), MOUTHPIECE (C), SKIPPING ROPE (D) AND BAG GLOVES (E).

Uniform and equipment

When you first start training, clubs are fairly flexible about dress requirements; a loose tracksuit or shorts and T-shirt are acceptable but you will be expected to get the correct uniform as soon as possible. Many clubs prescribe a set uniform to be worn for training on their premises but are flexible with regard to the colour and style of Muay Thai shorts to be worn for competitions.

A basic kit for training in Muay Thai consists of Thai boxing shorts, T-shirt, ankle supports, groin guard, mouthpiece, bag mitts and skipping ropes. Make sure you buy the authentic items as the bag mitts, for example, are specially designed for Muay Thai, being properly shaped to provide maximum comfort and support for the boxer's hands. Thai Boxing shorts, too, are wider in the leg to allow for kicking than the more restrictive style of international boxing shorts. Before buying any item of equipment always ask your instructor's advice.

Most clubs will provide the kicking pads, focus pads and usually boxing gloves for use during training, but it is always more beneficial to get your own boxing gloves rather than use a club pair that may have seen a hundred different hands inside them!

THE COACH'S EQUIPMENT FOR PAD WORK INCLUDES A BELLY PAD (A), SHIN GUARDS (B) AND LONG MITTS (C).

Muay Thai kicking pads, or long mitts (*Bao Thai*), are specifically designed for use by Thai boxers. They have three layers of high-density foam inside them, come in pairs and are worn strapped onto the forearm with a buckle or Velcro fastening. These should be worn with the buckles to the inside of the forearm to protect the boxer when kicking.

Focus pads, known in Western boxing as jab-and-hook mitts, are used in Muay Thai training to develop skill and accuracy in punching and elbow techniques. An abdominal protector, or belly pad (*Bao Tong*), is worn by the trainer with shin guards and long mitts. This kit is used by the trainer in freestyle pad work, allowing the boxer to practise the techniques with maximum power, while the trainer catches the techniques with the long mitts. When the trainer kicks the boxer, the shin guards protect the boxer from injury, while the belly pad is there for the fighter to practise the front kick (*teep*) and to protect the trainer if a knee or other technique misses the pads.

These items comprise the basic training equipment used in all Muay Thai schools.

Etiquette

The most important thing to remember when joining a club is to have the utmost respect for the teachers and for your fellow students. At your first class you will be taught how and when to bow (*wai*).

Clubs' regulations may differ in governing a student's behaviour. Here are the standard club rules:

■ Uniform must be worn according to the individually prescribed camp colour and must be kept in a clean condition.

■ Respect should be given to teachers and they should be called *Kru* or *Arjarn*.

■ Students must stand to attention when being spoken to or when speaking to teachers.

■ During training no valuables, such as rings, watches, necklaces or earrings, are to be worn.

■ *Wai* (bows) must be made to all instructors, seniors and training partners whenever entering or leaving the training room, and whenever a foul is struck during a training session.

■ No smoking in the presence of a teacher.

■ No alcohol is allowed before training.

■ No swearing is allowed.

■ Students must obtain permission to leave the training room during training.

■ Students are not allowed to train in other martial arts without the permission of their teacher.

■ Derogatory remarks should not be made about other martial arts and proper respect should be given to them.

■ All students must conduct themselves in a sportsmanlike manner.

■ Students must train regularly. If there are serious problems, then they should report to the teacher, otherwise they will not be allowed to train again.

■ Thai Boxing must not be used for a purpose that is against law and order.

THESE MUAY THAI STUDENTS IN THEIR TRAINING KIT.

Grading examinations

In Thailand there are no grading examinations for Muay Thai. This is purely a foreign innovation used because people in the West are accustomed to using some means of measuring their achievements in martial arts. Grading examinations are widely used in the UK, Europe and the USA.

The grading syllabus provides an accurate measure of progress at each stage. There are 10 grades in total and each stage is marked on technique, ritual dance, self-defence, rules and attendance. In addition, for Grades 5 and 6, the candidate will need to demonstrate combination techniques on a punch bag and/or freestyle pad work. In the higher grades of 7, 8 and 9, the student is also marked on knowledge of history, terminology, fighters' rules, the pledge, tactics and strategies. In the Instructor Grade (9), a student is also required to submit a written essay on the history of Muay Thai, organize a display or demonstration and must teach a class under the watchful eye of an examiner or technical committee.

In most martial arts when a student has passed a grading examination, they are awarded a belt or sash according to their grade. In Muay Thai, in keeping with the Thai tradition, the student is awarded a *Kruang Ruang (Pra Jer)* according to the grade attained (*see the photograph on the opposite page*). The colours of the *Kruang Ruangs* are as follows:

Grade 1	White
Grade 2	Yellow
Grade 3	Green
Grade 4	Blue
Grade 5	Blue with white stripe
Grade 6	Brown
Grade 7	Brown with white stripe
Grade 8	Brown with yellow stripe
Grade 9	Brown with green stripe
Grade 10	Red (instructor)
Senior/chief instructor	Red with white stripe

A Senior Instructor Grade is awarded when an instructor teaches another student up to Grade 9.

A chief instructor is somebody who has graded several students up to Grade 9 and is usually the proprietor of a camp or school.

Gradings are usually undertaken every three months but the student must have a minimum period of attendance for each grade. For the Instructor Grade, for example, a student must have trained on a regular basis for at least three years. In this way, a high standard is maintained in the martial art. This is also something a prospective student should ask about when looking for a good instructor. A good school only grades students when they have attained a high enough standard of practice for the grade they are sitting; so it doesn't mean that practitioners will necessarily take their grading examinations every three months.

Now that you've found the right school, welcome to the world of Muay Thai, Thai Boxing!

A pledge of honour

Every Thai boxer, in accordance with Thai tradition, is asked to make a pledge that can be either verbal or in a written format (usually inscribed in the licence book). This pledge would be made according to the following lines:

"I (name of student) hereby abide to uphold all the principles of Muay Thai and promise to honour the code of conduct taught by my teacher: *Arjarn/Kru* (name of particular teacher).

I will continue to promote and enhance the name of Muay Thai with great endeavour.

I will respect the laws and traditions of Muay Thai and I understand and appreciate that I am learning a potentially dangerous martial art. Therefore I promise not to use the art unless under extreme provocation where I might be compelled to defend myself, my family or friends or in support of law and order.

I will respect and honour my *Arjarn/Kru*, my seniors and my fellow students."

As students pass their grading examinations they are awarded a *Kruang Ruang*, otherwise known as *Pra Jer*, coloured according to the level of competency they have obtained.

IT IS ESSENTIAL TO WEAR GOOD QUALITY, PROPERLY FITTING EQUIPMENT WHEN PARTICIPATING IN MUAY THAI.

RITUALS AND TRADITIONS

There are many misconceptions about Muay Thai, one of which is that the *Wai Kru* and *Ram Muay* have religious connotations. This is not strictly true. The Wai Kru (respect-to-teacher ritual) is always followed by the *Ram Muay* (ritual dance). Both are essential parts of Muay Thai. Traditionally in Thailand, even before a prospective boxer was accepted as a student at a Muay Thai camp, he had to perform the *Yok Kru* ceremony (acceptance by the teacher). In Thailand today, many professional camps no longer adhere to this tradition but in provincial schools it is still an essential part of becoming a Muay Thai student.

The ceremony entails the prospective student learning a special *Wai Kru/Ram Muay* that he must perform for the teacher. In this way he shows his dedication to the camp and his willingness to learn by spending time studying and perfecting the dance without any guarantee that he will be accepted as a student. The prospective student will also make a small offering to the teacher. This usually consists of three joss sticks, a small piece of white cloth, one white flower, a candle and six or nine coins.

After making the offering the student will make a pledge to the teacher to never think or speak badly about the teacher or the school, or to make any remark that could damage the reputation of the teacher, school or fellow students.

The teacher will then accept the student as part of the school's family, after which he will then place a *Mongkon*, a sacred amulet, onto the student's head and will tie the *Pra Jer*, another sacred amulet, around his left bicep. The teacher will then confer a blessing on the boxer asking that no harm come to him, that he will never go hungry or thirsty, and that he never becomes seriously ill.

The *Mongkon* remains the property of the teacher while the *Pra Jer* is given to the boxer to keep. The next time the student will wear the *Mongkon* will be at his first fight. In modern Muay Thai camps today, the *Mongkon* and the *Pra Jer* are still essential parts of the pre-fight preparations.

Muay Thai is different from many other martial arts. The Thai boxer demonstrates his gratitude to his parents and teachers by performing the *Wai Kru* before every competition or bout. He acknowledges that it is his parents who gave him life and his teacher who gives him knowledge, without which he would have no existence. Muay Thai is not only about fighting. It is also about learning a skill with which to defend oneself, family, friends and country, and Muay Thai bouts are the methods by which skill and courage are tested.

Muay Thai students have a high standard to live up to, but this is what makes a genuine Muay Thai fighter, or *Nak Muay*, who is a gentleman in and out of the ring.

Take note of your elders' advice especially that of your teacher.

- Value yourself above money.
- Better to lose money than honour.
- Do not get angry.
- Be charitable and help others.
- Do not accept any illegal offers.
- Do not boast about your prowess in Muay Thai.
- Do not be vengeful; vengeance begets vengeance.
- Do not bully.
- Be loyal to your camp and peers.
- Be truthful in word and action.
- Be charitable and help others less fortunate than you.

opposite AN AMATEUR MUAY THAI BOXER PERFORMS THE *WAI KRU* (RESPECT-TO-TEACHER) RITUAL BEFORE COMPETING.

Wai Kru

The *Wai Kru* is always performed before every Muay Thai bout. *Wai Kru* literally means 'bow to teacher' but the words actually mean much more than that. The *Wai Kru* is a ceremony in which the fighter pays respect to his teacher and parents, and pays homage to the past masters of the art. Before the *Wai Kru*, the teacher will have placed the sacred *Mongkon* on the fighter's head, which enables spectators to discern where a fighter originates from and who his teacher is. An alternative means of doing so is to watch the *Wai Kru / Ram Muay*.

The *Pra Jer*, also known as the *Kruang Ruang*, is a piece of cotton cloth twisted, woven or plaited with magical symbols incorporated into it. A boxer might also add his own talismans, such as a lock of his mother's hair or an image of the Buddha to it.

Well-wishers also place flower garlands around a boxer's neck. In the past some boxers would have their bodies tattooed with magical prayers.

A boxer in full regalia is undoubtedly a formidable sight and can look quite daunting to an opponent. Nowadays, a tattooed boxer is rarely seen but the *Mongkon*, *Pra Jer* and garlands are a familiar sight at every Muay Thai bout.

The Mongkon

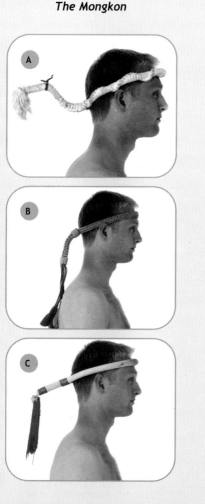

(a) When turned upward, the *mongkon* signifies that the fighter is a native of the south of Thailand.
(b) When it is pointing downward, it means the fighter is from the north of Thailand.
(c) When it is straight out, at a right angle to the back of the boxer's head, it signifies that he comes from the central plains.

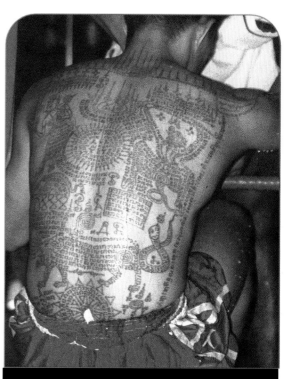

SACRED SYMBOLS TATTOOED ON A BOXER'S BACK PROVIDE SPIRITUAL PROTECTION DURING A BOUT.

How to perform the *Wai Kru*

⇐(A) Start by kneeling in a bowing (*wai*) position.

⇐(B) Place your left hand down to the floor.

⇐(C) Follow this up by placing your right hand on the ground, making a triangle shape with your hands.

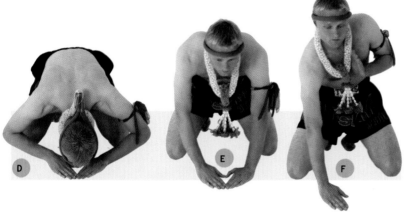

⇐(D) Place your head down between your two hands.

⇐(E) Raise your head.

⇐(F) Bring your left hand up.

⇐(G) Bring your right hand up to the bowing position.

⇐(H) Push up off the floor to a high kneeling position bringing your hands in a bowing position to the bridge of your nose.

⇐(I) Return to a low kneeling position; then repeat all of these movements three times.

Yang Sarm Khum

The *Yang Sarm Khum* is the basic footwork of Muay Thai. Its value is explained by a story from the *Ramakien*, the Thai version of the Indian epic story of good and evil, *Ramayana*:

The giant, Tatawan, was a diligent servant of the lord of the heavens, Shiva. As a reward, Shiva granted the giant 300 square miles of land where he could have complete omnipotence over all things. Unfortunately the giant then became very conceited, thinking he could do just as he liked. He began to devour everything that strayed on his land, even lesser gods and angels. Fear began to grow in heaven and everybody wanted him stopped. Shiva, heeding all the complaints, ordered Rama to rid the earth of the demon giant. Rama, a great strategist, disguised himself as a holy man and went to Tatawan's lands. When the demon giant confronted him, the holy man pretended to shake with fear and in a trembling voice asked: 'My lord I only want to perform a rite according to the book of Brahman. I did not intend to invade your privacy. Please have mercy, mighty one, and I will die willingly once I have finished my rite. All I need is a piece of ground which measures just three strides.'

The demon agreed to give the land but the holy man asked: 'My Lord will you later take the land back?' The demon replied: 'I am the ruler of this land and what I give is yours to keep.' Once the demon gave his

How to perform the Yang Sarm Khum

⇓(A) From the *Wai Kru,* come up to a standing position.

↘(B) From a standing position, begin the *Yang Sarm Khum.*

↘(C) In left guard take three steps to the left with your left leg, circling your hands three times with each step.

Dance with slow rhythmic movements highlighting your grace and balance, and breathe slowly in through your nose and out through your mouth to calm your nerves and increase the flow of oxygen into the bloodstream.

promise, Rama changed back to his mighty self, equal in size to the giant. The whole earth shook as Rama took three strides covering the whole of Tatawan's territory. Seeing Rama, the demon giant tried to flee, but having nowhere to run, was slain.

Similarly, in Muay Thai it is believed that once a boxer has perfected the *Yang Sarm Khum* footwork, there is no escape at all for his opponent.

In the *Yang Sarm Khum*, a boxer will circle his hands as he moves. Some believe this signifies him wrapping his hands in hemp rope, while others believe these movements originate from *Krabi Krabong* (Thai weapons art), when a warrior moves forward or backward defensively, circling his swords (*Daab*).

At the end of the *Wai Kru/Ram Muay*, and before removing the *mongkon*, the teacher will say a magic prayer or bestow a blessing over the boxer's head. The *pra-jer* remains around the boxer's arm. The *Mongkon*, however, is not allowed to be worn in modern Muay Thai bouts, but in the past, the *Mongkon* would either have remained positioned on the boxer's head or have been pulled down to sit around his neck while he fought his bout.

Throughout the execution of the *Wai Kru or Ram Muay*, a boxer cannot help but respond to the haunting sounds of the *Pi* (java pipe), the *Ching* (miniature cymbals) and the *Glawng Khaek* (drum) calling out their invitation to prepare for battle.

⇩(D)   Raise your right leg and swivel it, turning to the right.

↘(E)   You are now in the right guard position.

↘(F)   In the right guard, take three steps to the right with your right leg, circling your hands three times with each step. Repeat steps A to F three times in total.

Ram Muay

This is a vast and complex subject worthy of a volume on its own. There are literally hundreds of dances, every one taking a different form.

In Thailand each camp is instantly recognizable by the Ram Muay the boxer performs. By dancing a *Ram Muay*, a boxer is asking for the protection of the spirits during an upcoming battle. A *Ram Muay* is also a way for a boxer to warm up — the movements of the dance being used to stretch the muscles and tendons. It is also performed to show a boxer's prowess, good balance and control of movement and is used to warn opponents of imminent danger. Just as a monkey may pick up heavy rocks and thump the ground to show an adversary his strength and power, or a dog may raise its hackles and reveal its sharp fangs to a challenger, so too a boxer can use the *Ram Muay* to give an opponent a warning that today is not a good day to fight.

In the old days it is said that, if after watching the *Ram Muay*, a boxer felt that he had bitten off more than he could chew, he could bow out gracefully without actual, physical combat. Today bouts are professional, pre-arranged matches so, of course, a boxer would never bow out of a contest.

As the boxer begins the *Ram Muay* he will sometimes circle the ring sweeping a foot along the canvas. Some people say this signifies digging a grave for an opponent by knocking the soil away with the foot, but it's more likely that the boxer does this to test the ground on which he is to fight, gauging whether it is either dry and dusty, slippery or sticky. He will stop at each corner and *wai* (bow), asking for divine protection. By doing this he is not only sealing the ring from any outside influences but also sealing his opponent's fate!

Sometimes the *Ram Muay* will mimic the action of birds, such as the eagle or the swan in flight or even the peacock unfurling its tail. One can sometimes see the boxer take the form of the mythical *Garuda* in the four directions of the ring. The *Garuda* is a half-human, half-bird creature, which is said to guard against evil spirits. The *Garuda* has been a royal and national symbol of Thailand since 1868 and can often be seen on official buildings such as banks and government offices throughout Thailand. However, the dance usually depicts stories from the *Ramakien*.

top A CLASSICAL DEPICTION OF *RAMA* FIRING HIS MAGIC BOW. THIS FIGURE CAN BE FOUND IN THAI ARTS AND CRAFTS THROUGHOUT THE KINGDOM OF THAILAND.

left A THAI BOXER FROM SASIPRAPA CAMP IN BANGKOK PERFORMING THE *RAM MUAY* IN AMSTERDAM.

One of the most popular dances, and perhaps one of the most beautiful and elegant, is *Pra Rama Tam Gwang* or 'Lord Rama Hunts the Golden Deer'. The story on which the dance is based tells of the demon *Mareet* who transforms into a golden deer with diamond antlers such as has never been seen in the forest before. Sita, Rama's wife, spies on the creature in the forest and begs Rama to catch it for her. Despite his misgivings at leaving Sita alone, Rama sets out, equipped with his magic bow, to capture the animal. When this dance is performed, the boxer moves in a *Yang Sarm Khum* movement that depicts Rama striding through the forest.

During this dance a boxer may sometimes stop, raise his right hand to his brow as if looking for the golden deer, then, espying the animal, draw an imaginary arrow placing it in an imaginary bow. Raising one leg into the air the dancer unleashes the arrow, missing the target. His second attempt also fails. The boxer then raises his hands as if praying for divine intervention and, on the third attempt fires the arrow, successfully

striking the target. The boxer nods his head in approval, walks forward again in the *Yang Sarm Khum* movement and, lifting the fallen animal by its hooves, places it across his shoulders and walks back with the gift toward Sita in a *Yang Sarm Khum* movement.

By this ritual the boxer is warning his opponent that, just as Rama was successful in his quest, so too will he be victorious.

Other types of dances

Some dances mimic the actions of an ancient warrior sharpening an imaginary spear which is then launched at his opponent or into his corner. Others may depict a warrior making a bow and sharpening the arrowheads or forging a *daab* (Thai sword) with which to cut down his opponent. A more recent innovation is for a boxer to fire an imaginary gun at his opponent. Could these *Ram Muays* possibly prove the link to the Thai weapons art, Krabi Krabong?

BOXERS PERFORMING THE *RAM MUAY* AT BANGKOK'S RANGSIT STADIUM.

Pra Rama Tam Gwang

This ritual dance is preceded by the *Wai Kru* (p24) and the *Yang Sarm Khum* (p26). As explained on p29 this dance depicts the Lord Rama hunting the golden deer; a popular fable from the *Ramakien* and a story not only told in the Muay Thai ring but an all-time favourite in Thai classical dancing.

⇦(A) Look for the golden deer to the left.

⇲(B) Look for the golden deer to the right.

⇨(C) Circle your right hand backward over your head.

⇦(H) Place the arrow in the imaginary bow.

⇗(I) Take aim.

⇲(J) Release the arrow from the bow while, at the same time, the front foot comes down and the back foot comes up and out at 90 degrees from the hip. After releasing the arrow, perform the *Yang Sarm Khum* movement into your opponent's corner.

⇩(D) Stop your right hand just above the imaginary arrow quiver.

↘(E) Bring your hand down to draw the imaginary arrow from the quiver.

⇩(F) While drawing the arrow, your right foot moves forward from the back to join your left foot.

↘(G) As the arrow comes up out of the quiver, raise the front leg simultaneously.

⇩(K) Bend down to pick up the imaginary fallen deer.

↘(L) Place the deer across your shoulders. At this stage, perform the *Yang Sarm Khum* in reverse.

⇨(M) Salute by politely bowing your head to finish the dance.

PHYSICAL INFORMATION

Exercise, Diet and Weight Loss

To participate in Muay Thai, practitioners require many skills, the most important of these being strength, stamina, speed, suppleness and strategy. Secondary skills that are acquired as a result of practice are good coordination, rhythm, timing and balance, all of which contribute to successful participation in the art. Here is a detailed look at these contributing factors.

■ **Strength**

Strength is developed in the muscles and tendons to support the bone structure and protect it from injury when practising on pads or bags.

■ **Stamina**

Muay Thai is an endurance sport. For a novice competitor, who has to stay active for three two-minute periods, through to a top-class competitor who is constantly active for five three-minute periods, stamina is an essential element of this activity.

■ **Speed**

As with all active sports, speed is a vital constituent. In Muay Thai speed allows the boxer to react quicker in defensive or offensive situations.

■ **Suppleness**

Suppleness is essential to enable the boxer to perform a technique to the highest possible level without injury to the muscles and tendons.

■ **Strategy**

Muay Thai can be likened to a game of chess and requires a game plan. A competitor needs to out-think his opponent so that he can utilize his best techniques with maximum effectiveness.

■ **Coordination**

Coordination is an important skill to have in Muay Thai, particularly for executing combinations in which the boxer is using every part of his body simultaneously.

■ **Rhythm**

Rhythm is essential so that the techniques in Muay Thai can be executed fluently.

■ **Timing**

The correct timing gives power and accuracy in the execution of techniques, allowing for maximum effect with minimum effort.

■ **Balance**

Good balance aids the execution of techniques and ability to defend. In balance one can attack and defend in quick succession but, if one is off-balance, defence is not possible and leaves one open to counterattack.

Some of these skills are inherent in all individuals but the initial warming-up period of any class will include exercises and activities designed to enhance the student's natural attributes. An instructor can assess each student taking into account his or her strengths and weaknesses with regards to these skills and direct their training accordingly, thus ensuring that the student becomes a well-rounded practitioner of the art.

In an average class of one to one-and-a-half hours, the student will spend 20 to 30 minutes doing stretching and strength-building warm-up exercises. The lesson will then progress to the actual techniques of kicking, punching, knee and elbow techniques, and combinations of these. Each lesson becomes different at this stage but the three main areas include pad, partner and bag work. Techniques are practised for 45 to 50 minutes followed by 10 to 15 minutes of light free-sparring and warm-down exercises.

opposite BOXERS FROM SASIPRAPA CAMP ON A DAWN RUN THROUGH THE STREETS OF BANGKOK.

Exercise

A normal class warm-up will consist of exercises that serve to warm up the body, helping speed up circulation and the flow of oxygen to the muscles. These exercises include skipping, shadow boxing and jogging on the spot. Strengthening exercises help to build up strength and endurance in the muscles and tendons. They also prepare the body to absorb the impact and stress of the prescribed regimen. Strengthening exercises might include sit-ups, press-ups, calf raises, squats, dips and leg raises. Finally the warm-up may incorporate stretching exercises of a yoga or gymnastic nature similar to other martial arts. These serve to increase the practitioner's range of movement; help prevent strains and sprains; and prepare the body for strenuous activity. Stretching exercises would normally include heel-and-toe touches, twists, pelvic tilts and circles, leg stretches and flexes. Some exercises are also done with a partner. This adds more weight to the session and thus greater resistance to any exercise. These might include squats and calf raises, clinch work and advanced stretching. With so many subsidiary fitness activities such as running, skipping, swimming, stretching exercises and meditation incorporated into Muay Thai training, in addition to the core techniques, the benefits to the health and wellbeing of participating individuals are incalculable. Physically the heart-lung-circulation fitness, muscle endurance and strength, coordination, and flexibility are all vastly enhanced while mental relaxation is achieved by means of short periods of meditation incorporated into the *Ram Muay,* or ritual-dance, movements.

Strengthening exercises

Squats

⇦(A) Stand straight with your feet apart and your hands locked behind your head.

⇨(B) Keeping your back straight, bend your knees until in a squatting position, with your knees bent at right angles to your lower legs. Repeat A and B continuously.

Sit-ups

(A) Lie down with your feet and back flat on the floor, knees bent and your hands interlocked behind your head, which is raised.

(B) Keeping your feet flat on the floor and your hands behind your head, use your stomach muscles to raise your body upward. Move your chest to your knees. Repeat A and B continuously.

Advanced students and fighters perform strengthening exercises during rest periods, between rounds or with a partner to increase weight and resistance in the execution of their techniques. These exercises include squats, sit-ups and press-ups. When starting these exercises begin slowly at your own pace doing 10 to 15 of each, increasing gradually until you can do between 50 and 75.

Press-ups

(A) Lie down with your chest to the floor. Bring your arms at right angles to your body, placing your hands palm-down.

(B) Raise your body by pushing up on your arms until fully extended while keeping your body straight. Repeat A and B continuously.

Stretching exercises

It's important to stretch before doing Muay Thai. Remember, when stretching, not to rush and not to bounce. Stretch gradually to a comfortable pull on the muscles, hold for 10 seconds, then relax and repeat. Before doing any stretching ensure your body is warm by doing light jogging on the spot, skipping or by rubbing Thai Boxing liniment on the muscles.

Stretching is very important because the more flexible and supple you are, the more fluently you will be able to execute the techniques.

Inner-thigh stretches

This exercise stretches the inner thigh as well as the hamstring of the extended leg and the outer thigh of the bent leg.

⇐ Squat low down to the floor, bending one leg and keeping the other stretched out sideways at right angles to the body. Keep both feet flat on the floor, then move from left to right, bending and straightening your legs as appropriate. Hold each of the stretches for 10 seconds.

This exercise is slightly different and aims at stretching the hamstring more.

⇐Squat low down on the floor in a similar position to the previous exercise. Pull the toe of your left leg up and back toward your body. Hold this position for 10 seconds, then change and repeat this on the other leg.

⇓(A) Sit on the floor with your back straight. Tuck your right leg into the inner thigh of your left leg. Stretch the left leg out at approximately 135 degrees to the body with your toes pointing up.

⇓(B) Bend forward, keeping your right thigh and calf flat on the floor, and stretch to touch the toe of your left leg. Hold for 10 seconds, then repeat the stretch on the other leg.

A

B

Upper-thigh stretches

⇧(A) From a standing position, with your legs as far apart as possible, your feet flat on the floor and without bending your knees, bend from the hips and twist to touch your left foot.

⬀(B) Repeat, this time touching your right foot.

⇨(C) This time push your arms out as far forward as possible. Hold for 10 seconds, then repeat A, B and C.

> *These exercises are good for stretching the inside thighs, the hamstring and lower back.*

⬿(A) Sit on the floor with your legs as wide apart as possible. Without bending your knees and keeping your legs flat on the floor, bend to touch your left foot bringing your body down over and along your left leg.

⬿(B) Repeat, this time to the right side.

⬇(C) This time push your arms forward as far out as possible. Try to bring your body flat to the floor, keeping your legs straight.

Trunk turns

This exercise strengthens the hips and lower back. It is used a lot in Muay Thai and is also good for firming and toning the waistline.

⇐(A) Stand straight with your arms at right angles to your body. Bend your elbows and link your hands in front of your chest.

⇐(B) Keeping one foot flat on the ground and your arms in the same position as A, twist your body to the right.

⇒(C) Then, twist to the left.

Advanced inner-thigh stretch

⇐(A) Sit on the floor with your legs as wide apart as possible. Your partner should stand behind you. Without bending your knees and keeping your legs flat on the floor, bend to touch your left foot bringing your body down over and along your leg. Your partner should then position both his hands on your lower back and apply gentle pressure to enable you to stretch further.

(B) Repeat, this time to the right side with your partner once again applying gentle pressure to push you further.

(C) This time push your arms forward as far out as possible. Try to bring your body flat to the floor keeping your legs straight. This should be made easier to do as once again your partner applies gentle pressure to your lower back. Complete three to five sets of this exercise before allowing your partner a turn.

Diet

It is important that students do not eat at least two hours before training and do not drink at least one hour before training. They should always try to eat small meals at regular intervals and never eat late at night. Rice or pasta, a little white meat, fish, vegetables and fruit are ideal. Bread or potatoes, sugary drinks, sweets or fatty foods are not allowed and alcohol is strictly forbidden. Red meat is to be avoided.

Before a competition, it is important for practitioners to build up reserves of energy. These foods will help the boxer reduce his weight while enabling him to maintain a perfect level of fitness. Remember, during intensive training, the body uses a large amount of energy, so a boxer will also need plenty of carbohydrates. A little protein will help him maintain his musculature without accumulating fatty deposits. Drinking water will also help to maintain balance and flush out impurities leaving his body perfectly conditioned. With the correct diet and training programme, a boxer will not need any food supplements.

Weight loss

Training hard and maintaining this type of diet will cause a boxer to automatically lose weight. He should, however, do so gradually, failing which he may experience a rapid loss of energy leading to fatigue and poor performance in competitions. A boxer should remember to refrain from eating or drinking 24 hours before a weigh-in so as to achieve maximum results. (Note: a weigh-in should take place 12 to 24 hours before the start of a competition.)

To a lesser extent massage is another method of assisting weight loss. In having the muscles massaged with Thai boxing oil (*Nam Mun Muay*) before training, the blood begins to circulate faster causing the muscles to heat up. Thus the boxer will begin to sweat rapidly once exercise commences. Some believe massage also helps accelerate the break up of fatty deposits in the body thereby assisting the boxer to shed weight more quickly.

This information is more specifically for Muay Thai competitors who fight in weight divisions, where they try to stay in the lowest division possible, but is also suitable for any student wishing to lose weight during their training in Muay Thai. Obviously when using this type of regimen purely to reduce weight the 12 to 24-hour period of abstinence would be unnecessary.

FRESH FRUIT IS A MUST FOR ALL ATHLETES AS IT IS AN ESSENTIAL SOURCE OF VITAMINS AND MINERALS.

MUAY THAI TECHNIQUES

Muay Thai utilizes nine weapons: two hands, two elbows, two knees, two legs and the head. Some scholars believe that the ninth weapon, the head, was used for attacking in the days when head butting was permitted but, in fact, the head is the most important weapon of all because it contains the brain: essential for outmanoeuvering and outsmarting one's opponent.

The guard

The emphasis in the Muay Thai guarding position is to protect the head at all times, the head being the control tower for the rest of the body. Muay Thai has a left guarding position and a right guarding position.

Yang Sarm Khum

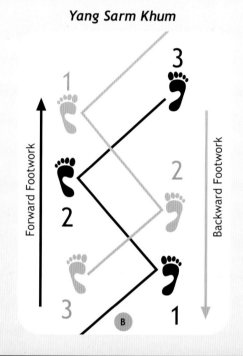

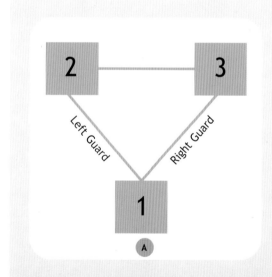

THE ORTHODOX LEFT GUARDING POSITION ENTAILS THE RIGHT FOOT BEING POSITIONED ON 1, AND THE LEFT FOOT BEING POSITIONED ON 2. THE SOUTHPAW RIGHT GUARDING POSITION ENTAILS THE LEFT FOOT BEING POSITIONED ON 1, AND THE RIGHT FOOT ON 3.

THE RULES WITH FORWARD AND BACKWARD MOVEMENT ARE:

■ TO MAINTAIN A SAFE DISTANCE (1).

■ FOR POWER IN A TECHNIQUE, THROWN FROM THE RIGHT, MAKE A FORWARD SIDE-STEP WITH YOUR LEFT FOOT TO THE LEFT (2).

■ FOR POWER IN A TECHNIQUE, THROWN FROM THE LEFT, MAKE A FORWARD SIDE-STEP WITH YOUR RIGHT FOOT TO THE RIGHT (3).

■ TO EVADE A TECHNIQUE, COMING FROM THE LEFT, MAKE A BACKWARD SIDE-STEP WITH YOUR RIGHT FOOT TO THE RIGHT (2).

■ TO EVADE A TECHNIQUE, COMING FROM THE RIGHT, MAKE A BACKWARD SIDESTEP WITH YOUR LEFT FOOT TO THE LEFT (3).

opposite WHEN AN OPPONENT (RIGHT) THROWS A CIRCULAR ELBOW, THE BOXER LEANS BACK AND JAMS HIS OPPONENT'S HAND OR WRIST WITH ONE HAND; THE OTHER HAND PRESSES DOWN ON HIS OPPONENT'S BICEP OR ELBOW WHICH DISLOCATES THE SHOULDER.

The position of the hands gives the boxer greater protection around his head while his forearms and elbows protect his body. Either his right or left leg can be raised to block with the shin, thus protecting either his thighs or calves. After executing or blocking, parrying or evading any technique, the boxer should always resume the guarding position, constantly moving while maintaining a good defensive posture.

A good analogy for this can be found in warfare; you have a base camp that is protected at all times and from which you plan strategies and tactics. The guarding position is the base camp of Muay Thai wherein the boxer feels secure and able to think clearly, planning his following tactics and strategies.

> *You should never bring your feet too close together nor too far apart. You should also never stand square-on to your opponent.*

Yang Sarm Khum

Muay Thai footwork all relates to the *Yang Sarm Khum*, three-sectioned footwork. Diagram A (*see* p40) shows the basic standing guard positions while diagram B illustrates the forward and backward footwork.

Moving in *Yang Sarm Khum* allows the boxers to move at a 45-degree angle rendering it more difficult for their opponents to attack them. It's easier to hit something moving in a straight line than something moving diagonally from side to side. Take, for instance, a rabbit or hare avoiding capture by a predator; he runs in a zigzag pattern, known in Muay Thai as the *Yang Sarm Khum*. A boxer should carefully study the footwork of the *Yang Sarm Khum* in order to become proficient at it. Good *Yang Sarm Khum* footwork keeps the boxer in perfect balance; ready to attack or defend at any moment.

The guard

In both the left ⇦(A) and right guarding position ⇨(B), your front hand should be forward and slightly higher than the rear hand with your shoulder slightly raised to protect your chin. The top of the front fist should be level with your eyebrows and the top of the rear fist level with the centre of your ear. This protects your jaw and balance canals in the inner ear. Your elbows should be kept low to cover your floating ribs.

Your body weight should be concentrated on the balls of your feet, distributed equally between your front and rear legs. Keep your heels very light, allowing you to move quickly. This will also allow you to pivot easily when delivering or blocking techniques. Your legs should be positioned at 45 degrees to one another, allowing you to use both legs either for defensive or offensive manouevres.

The left guard

The right guard

Fighting distance

In Muay Thai the legs are the long-range weapons used to keep an opponent at bay or to attack from a distance. The hands are the medium-range weapons used for boxing an opponent, while the knees and elbows are used in close-range fighting. There are, of course, exceptions to this rule. A knee can be used when jumping to cover a great distance, as can an elbow or a punch. Kicks can be used at medium- or short-range distances using the upper shin as the attacking area.

The fighting distances in Muay Thai:

- **Half a step** forward allows the boxer to deliver his kicks, front kick (*teep*) or round kick (*daet*), to any part of the body.
- **One full step** allows the boxer to use his hands to box his opponent.
- **One-and-a-half** steps allows the boxer to effectively use his knee.
- **Two full steps** brings the boxer close enough to use his elbows on his opponent.

A boxer must know the correct techniques to use for every situation. He can learn this through constant pad work in which the trainer can change distances quickly. For example, if the trainer were to move in toward the boxer suddenly, he would need to know which technique to use at this distance; either the knee or elbow. If the trainer were to step back quickly the boxer would need to follow him, maintaining an appropriate fighting distance and delivering the correct striking technique.

So as one can see, to deliver an elbow strike — considered to be the most dangerous technique in Muay Thai — the boxer would need to cover a greater distance. Constant practice with a trainer holding the pads will improve a boxer's fighting distance, enabling him to stay just out of range of the trainer's attacks but able to come into range quickly to deliver his attacks before retreating back to safety. The boxer can stay at a safe distance by continuously front kicking (*teep*) to the abdominal protector worn around the trainer's mid-section.

Not only would pad work improve a boxer's fighting techniques at various ranges but it would also help him improve his timing. This is because the trainer moves at different speeds and angles, making it difficult for the boxer. Pad work would also increase the boxer's strength, stamina and endurance as every technique is delivered to the pads with maximum power and precise timing and distance.

Alternatively, for training at home a punch or kick bag can be used, although this is not as beneficial as pad work because these bags are relatively static. They do, nevertheless, help with developing power, timing and footwork.

Conditioning

Constantly striking the pads and the kick bag conditions the body. The long mitt (*Bao Thai*) can also be used for this purpose. Having a partner strike your upper thigh will help condition the muscle. Another conditioning exercise is for you to raise your leg into a blocking position while your partner repeatedly strikes your shin with the pad. This not only helps to condition the shin but also helps to improve your balance when blocking.

The pad can also be used to strike the forearms and upper arms, and when in the reclining position of a sit-up, can be used to strike the stomach. Another option in this latter position, is to frequently drop a medicine ball onto your stomach to condition the abdominal muscles. For practice at home, use your clenched hands to repeatedly strike around your thighs while you squat.

Free sparring is another method of conditioning the body. It is never done with maximum power but should be hard enough to condition the body without causing bruising or injury.

A great constituent of conditioning is mental attitude; only by pushing yourself further through the pain barrier will you become inured to pain.

Breathing and timing

An exhalation of air should always accompany the execution of a technique. Before throwing the technique the boxer will inhale through the nose. As he strikes, the air is pushed downward toward his lower abdomen; this causes the excess air to be expelled explosively through his mouth. The *iiiish* sound made when expelling the air is the audible trademark of every Muay Thai camp.

The correct breathing can improve the power of a technique by up to 100%. Breathing and timing go hand in hand. Both are perfected by constant practice as the boxer forces the air downward at the exact moment of impact. In Thailand one often sees young boxers practising punching techniques on a lime or tennis ball suspended at eye-level from a string above their heads. Not only does this help the co-ordination between the eye and the body but also, when the correct timing and breathing are achieved, the object being punched will shoot up into the air with very little effort on the part of the boxer.

Correct breathing is also an asset in clinch work. When a boxer pushes the air down into his lower abdomen and then locks his stomach muscles, it makes him heavier. When executing a clinch, this makes it more difficult for his opponent to move. Remember a jackhammer uses only compressed air to drive it and this very air can smash solid concrete to a million pieces. So to get the maximum effect from a technique with minimum effort, it is essential to have the correct breathing, timing, footwork and fighting distance. All Muay Thai techniques are delivered through the target area, firstly to increase impact and secondly in anticipation of the opponent trying to move out of range.

Boxing (*Doi Mat*)

Before the introduction of boxing gloves, fighters would wrap their hands in hemp rope, which would form small knots across the knuckles of the hand and up and down the inside and outside of the forearm similar to the chainmail used by knights of old. Punching then differed from modern methods in that the hands were used to slash or cut as well as to deliver heavy knock-out blows. This type of fighting was outlawed more than 80 years ago but it still exists on the borders of Thailand and Burma.

Punches

Today most Thai boxers opt to use Western-style boxing techniques as the most commonly used punches in Muay Thai. These techniques originate from international boxing, thus they retain their English names such as the jab, hook and uppercut.

Statistically the most common knockout in a Muay Thai ring is caused by hand strikes in the form of either a right cross or a left hook. All Muay Thai techniques can deliver a knockout blow but, in general, the elbow is more dangerous with regard to cuts; the knee and kicking techniques are utilized to weaken an opponent with boxing techniques delivering the *coup de grâce*.

To become proficient in boxing techniques you need to practise shadow boxing with hand weights, approximately 1kg(2 lb) in weight. For speed, it is important to train in pad work using the focus pads (jab and hook mitts) for power and timing. Make the most of a heavy punch bag to strengthen both your hands and upper body so that you will be able to deliver more powerful punches.

Note: Thai boxers fight from guards, southpaw and orthodox, but for the purposes of this book all the techniques will be shown using the left or orthodox guarding position (*see* p42).

Traditional principles

Traditionally Muay Thai has many ways of attacking using the hand or forearm. Many of the old techniques, although still legal in the modern sport, are rarely utilized. These include Erawan Soi Naga, a very long uppercut punch, and Hanuman Tawai Wen, a two-handed uppercut. These, and many other traditional techniques in Muay Thai, as with the *Ram Muay* ritual dances, depict stories from the *Ramakien*.

Some of the other hand techniques also trace their origins from Krabi Krabong (Thai weapons art). When a warrior lost his weapons he would use his body's

Basic punches

⇦Jab punch

The jab is always thrown from the front hand and can be used as a method of setting your opponent up so that you can throw the cross, or as a way of disrupting his concentration by constantly jabbing his eyes or nose.

⇨Straight punch (cross)

A powerful punch, the straight punch is delivered from the rear hand and picks up momentum. By twisting your body and hips you can throw your whole body weight into it.

⇨The hook punch

A hook can be delivered powerfully from the front or rear hand by stepping in its direction, twisting your whole body and keeping your elbow and shoulder level with your hand.

⇦The uppercut

The uppercut can be delivered with the front or rear hand. To generate power, use your legs: bend your knees, push up with your legs and use your shoulder to drive it.

⇦Stepping punch

Step forward quickly with the rear leg, simultaneously using your rear hand to deliver a punch that should strike your target a split second before your foot lands. This puts your full body weight behind the strike.

⇨Jumping punch

From the guarding position take a short step forward with the front leg; jump into the air bringing the rear leg forward, then kick it backward and deliver a punch from the same side.

natural armature: hands, feet, knees and elbows, following the same principles as the weapons' system. A perfect example of this is the spinning back fist. Man is a hunter but unlike most predators, humans don't have claws, tusks, horns or sharp teeth with which to hunt. From the beginnings of martial arts humans have studied animals to learn their fighting methods and have incorporated their tactics into their fighting arts. This is apparent in Muay Thai and in the Cobra adaptation, in particular (*see* below).

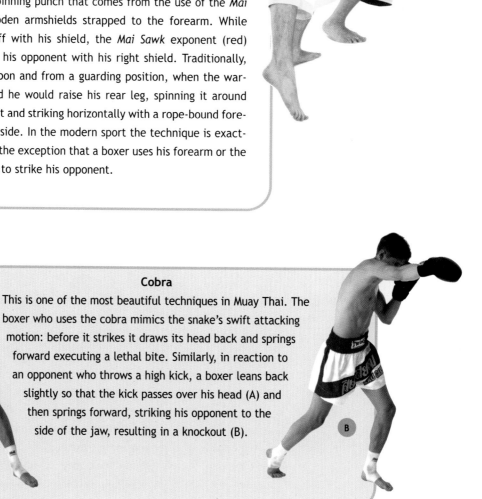

The evolution of a punch

A perfect example of a hand technique that has evolved from Krabi Krabong is the spinning punch that comes from the use of the *Mai Sawk*, small wooden armshields strapped to the forearm. While blocking the staff with his shield, the *Mai Sawk* exponent (red) spins and strikes his opponent with his right shield. Traditionally, without the weapon and from a guarding position, when the warrior was attacked he would raise his rear leg, spinning it around from back to front and striking horizontally with a rope-bound forearm of the same side. In the modern sport the technique is exactly the same with the exception that a boxer uses his forearm or the back of his glove to strike his opponent.

Cobra

This is one of the most beautiful techniques in Muay Thai. The boxer who uses the cobra mimics the snake's swift attacking motion: before it strikes it draws its head back and springs forward executing a lethal bite. Similarly, in reaction to an opponent who throws a high kick, a boxer leans back slightly so that the kick passes over his head (A) and then springs forward, striking his opponent to the side of the jaw, resulting in a knockout (B).

A

B

Defences

⇧Parrying the jab

When an opponent throws a jab, slip to the right parrying it with your right hand. Parry across rather than down to prevent a right-cross from your opponent. The opposite applies for a southpaw opponent.

⇧Parrying the right-cross

When an opponent throws a right-cross, slip your body to the left, using your left hand to parry the punch. Parry across to prevent your opponent delivering a left hook. The opposite applies for a southpaw opponent.

⇧Defence against a left hook

When your opponent throws a left hook raise your right hand high so that your elbow is in line with your chin. Make sure your arm covers your chin and right ear. The opposite applies for a southpaw opponent.

⇧Defence against a right uppercut

Lean back, chin down and left hand below it. The right hand jams the opponent's left arm at the inner elbow. This stops the punch and overbalances the opponent. The opposite applies for a southpaw opponent.

Wrapping your hands

As your punching power increases, it is important to protect your hands properly using a gauze bandage and material tape, particularly when you are practising boxing techniques on the heavy punch bags. Firmly wrapping the hands, and applying the bandage approximately 5cm(2in) along the wrists will help support the small bones. It is vital that the bandage fits between the fingers and the thumb as these can be knocked back when parrying or catching kicks. The knuckles need to be well padded by wadding the bandage over and across the knuckles. This builds a cushion that protects the hands. In Muay Thai it is important that the palm is unhindered by bandaging, enabling the boxer to close his hands properly.

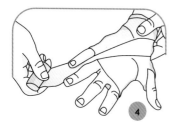

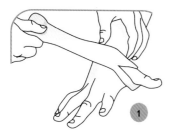

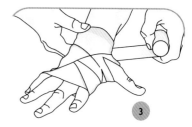

⇧(1) Make an incision at the end of the bandage and place the thumb through the opening.

⇧(2) Bind across the knuckles and then around the wrist and across the hand.

⇧(3) Go back around the hand from left to right and right to left.

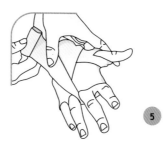

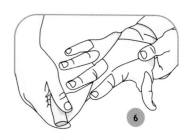

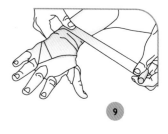

⇧(4) Wrap each finger; the little finger first.

⇧(5) Wrap the third finger, the back of the hand and the wrist.

⇧(6) Come back across and between the middle and index fingers.

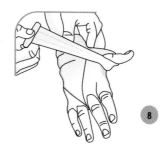

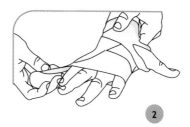

⇧(7) Loop up around the index finger, down the back of the hand and around the wrist.

⇧(8) Encircle the thumb, up around the wrist and across the hand.

⇧(9) Wrap the bandage around the wrist again.

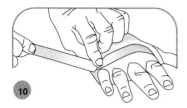

⇧(10) Use the bandage to wad across the knuckles to protect them.

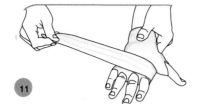

⇧(11) Wrap the bandage once across the knuckles to hold the wadding in place, then around into the palm of the hand, tucking the end inside itself.

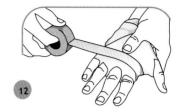

⇧(12) Wrap soft surgical tape at least twice around the knuckles to further secure the wadding.

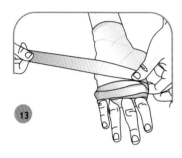

⇧(13) Cut another piece of tape twice the width of the hand; fold in half revealing a sticky lip and secure half its width across the knuckles.

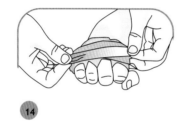

⇧(14) Do this several times to build up firm protection around the knuckles.

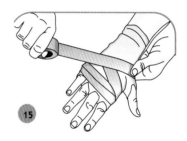

⇧(15) Wrap tape firmly around the padding to secure it to the bandage.

⇧(16) Wrap the tape around wrist and hand several times, crisscrossing it for added support.

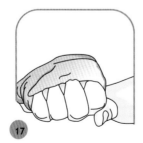

⇧(17) The knuckles and hand will now be well protected.

⇧(18) It's important that the palm be left open so that the boxer can close his hands properly.

Elbows (*Sawk*)

The elbow is undoubtedly the most formidable weapon in Muay Thai; the skill of skills when used correctly. It is a misconception that the elbow is only an attacking weapon. Surprisingly, it is one of the most effective methods of blocking an opponent. In the past it was often said that Thai boxers were made of granite because every time an opponent struck he would hurt himself. This was because the Thai boxers were very skilful in the defensive use of their elbows and were actually blocking attacks with elbow techniques. For instance, when a punch was thrown, the Thai boxer would block it by raising his arm. The punch would clash with the elbow, damaging the opponent's hand. Alternatively, when attacked by a kick, the Thai boxer would angle his body so that his elbow would either meet the opponent's shin or instep.

The elbow can be delivered in nine directions:

- Straight across at 90^0 to strike the left side of the opponent's head
- Straight across at 90^0 to strike the right side of the opponent's head
- Downward at 90^0 to strike the centre top of the opponent's head
- Upward at 90^0 to strike centrally under the opponent's jaw
- Downward at 45^0 to strike the top left side of the opponent's head
- Downward at 45^0 to strike the top right side of the opponent's head
- Upward at 45^0 to strike the left side of the opponent's jaw
- Upward at 45^0 to strike the right side of the opponent's jaw
- Straight forward in a horizontal line to strike the opponent's nose

* These strikes can also be delivered to any part of the body

Elbow techniques

Elbow techniques can be delivered using either the left or right arm.

Side-strike elbow

Keeping light on your feet, step forward with your left foot. Raise your shoulder and, with the elbow at 90 degrees to the torso, twist your whole body, keeping your head still and your eyes fixed on the target. Strike with the left elbow. It is important to keep your right hand high covering your temple, as your opponent could strike with the same technique.

Circular elbow

From a guarding position, raise yourself high on your toes. Lift your shoulder high, tucking the arm under. Making a circular anti-clockwise movement close to your opponent's head, strike with the point of your elbow.

The elbow can be delivered in nine directions (*see* panel opposite). There are also two ways to deliver the strikes. The first is using the elbow with the fist clenched and delivering a solid blow, usually used to cause a knockout. The second requires great precision and timing, and is delivered with the hand open, the elbow barely skimming the surface of the opponent's skin, causing a laceration similar to a knife or razor cut. These elbows are usually delivered to just above the opponent's eyes to cause bleeding which runs into the eyes. This interferes with the opponent's vision thereby ending the contest with a technical knockout (TKO). In the early days when bouts were fought until first blood was drawn, the boxer who was skilful with the elbow could gain victory very quickly. Even today Thai boxers worldwide are not keen to fight an opponent renowned for his skill with the elbow! Although an elbow strike is thought to be dangerous, a Thai boxer can only deliver such a technique once he gets past six other weapons: the legs, hands and knees.

To do so, not only does a boxer need to be proficient with elbow techniques, he must also have good footwork and exceptional tactical ability. This is why the use of elbow techniques is considered

Straight uppercut elbow

Stepping forward with your knees slightly bent, rise up on your toes, in a similar manner as in the uppercut punch. Raise the elbow upward at 90 degrees to the torso, stretch the whole body upward for maximum power, striking with the point of your elbow. As with all elbow techniques this is a short-range weapon so you need to start the move with a feint, possibly a jab. This disguises the fact that you intend to move in closer to your opponent in order to use your elbows.

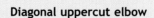

Diagonal uppercut elbow

This strike is similar to the straight uppercut elbow except that the elbow moves across diagonally at 45 degrees. This technique often precedes a knee strike; after hitting with the elbow, the arm comes down, gripping the back of the opponent's neck to deliver the knee.

the skill of skills. Many countries outside Thailand do not permit the use of the elbow to the head in C- and B-class contests. Only in A-class championship level bouts, when a boxer has become sufficiently skilled and experienced, will the trainer allow the boxer to fight using the full range of Muay Thai techniques. These include the side-strike elbow, uppercut elbow, circular elbow, jumping downward-strike elbow, reverse elbow and the jumping side-strike elbow.

In Thailand it is said that unless all of the techniques are used, the practice is not classified as a pure form of Muay Thai. In the rest of the world, however, Muay Thai is relatively new and so the boxers don't have the many generations' experience necessary to successfully compete at the same level as their Thai counterparts until they reach 'A' class, although nowadays the West is quickly catching up!

To become proficient in elbow techniques it is necessary to condition the elbows by hitting them repeatedly against a heavy punch bag, but a maize ball is preferable. This causes the bone around the elbow joint to thicken. One can also practise elbow strikes on focus pads, which helps with developing speed, co-ordination and timing. Interestingly, women are better equipped for these techniques, firstly because they have better mobility in their shoulders than men, and secondly because their elbows taper to a sharp point.

⬀Jumping downward strike elbow

This technique is known as 'Hanuman Catches the Stars'. Take one small step forward with your left leg, and leap into the air, raising your right arm straight upward as if grasping a star. Then pull your arm down sharply to strike with the point of the elbow. This technique can be directed at the top of an opponent's head and cause a knockout or lacerations. The power in this technique is generated by your weight which is brought down by gravity at the same time as your elbow. This is one of the most feared techniques in Muay Thai.

⬀Jumping side-strike elbow

This technique is executed in exactly the same way as a jumping punch. From a left guarding position, take a short step forward with your left leg, then jump into the air bringing the rear leg forward; kick it backward, simultaneously delivering a side-strike elbow with your right arm.

Defences against elbow strikes

The best defence against any elbow technique is the front kick (*teep*). This will keep the opponent constantly at a long-range distance where he will be unable to use any elbow techniques.

⇨**Defence against reverse elbow strike**

The reverse elbow strike is dangerous as it can catch a boxer unawares. The opponent (white shorts) side-steps and quickly twists his body to strike with his elbow. To defend this, block the back of the attacking arm with your forearm, and counter with a straight uppercut elbow to the opponent's back.

⇧**Defence against circular elbow strike**

As your opponent throws a circular elbow aimed for the top of your head, quickly lean away, jamming the hand of his striking arm against his body; then add to the opponent's momentum by pressing down on top of his elbow. This can cause damage to the opponent's shoulder and cause him to lose balance. This is a classical Muay Thai technique known as 'Breaking the Crane's Wing'.

Knees (*Kao*)

The basic knee techniques of Muay Thai include the straight knee, side knee, small knee, flying knee, clinch and straight knee, and clinch and side knee. The use of the knee is the second most feared technique in Muay Thai, second only to the elbow. Whenever Thai boxers fight against practitioners of other martial arts in Thailand or abroad, the two main techniques used against opponents will involve the elbow and knee. When a Thai boxer holds his opponent, this renders the opponent defenceless and unable to deliver kicks or punches. This gives the boxer the advantage of following up using short-range knee and elbow techniques.

In the early days of Muay Thai, clinch work played a minor part in the overall techniques used. It was only in the late 1960s and early 1970s that this aspect of Muay Thai developed into an important asset. Today, the older, more traditional boxers don't approve of clinching. However, modern boxers appreciate that there is great skill involved in good clinch work, the theory behind it being to use your opponent's strength against himself and to unbalance him to deliver a devastating knee either to his body or head.

⇨Clinch and straight knee

Hold your opponent strongly around his neck with one hand clasped over the other. Staying on your toes, bring the leg you wish to strike with back and, while jerking your opponent's head downward, throw it upward at either 45 degrees to strike his body with your knee or vertically at 90 degrees to deliver a strike to his head.

⇦Clinch and side knee

This technique is easy to deliver when your opponent attempts to clinch and hold you closely in order to nullify your techniques. Hold your opponent's neck in the same way as in the straight knee technique, clasping one hand over the other. Deliver the knee strike in a circular movement, striking with the point of the knee to the opponent's body.

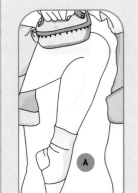

Knee strikes

There are two methods of striking with the knee. Some schools prefer a knee strike to be delivered with the toe pointing down and backward so as to make the knee into a very fine point (A). This method pulls the ligaments tightly across the knee, giving the joint full support.

The other method is quite an old-style strike, in which the toe points out at right angles to the shin (B). If the boxer misses his target with the knee, he will then be able to follow up with the ball of the foot pushing outward, striking his opponent's lower thigh just above the knee. This technique is known as 'The Chicken Pecks'.

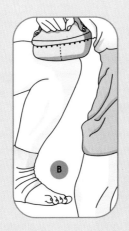

⇦**Straight knee**

The front knee is delivered in the same manner as in the clinch and straight knee technique but without holding the opponent's neck. Using your back leg, drive your knee forward and upward. This is very effective when used in conjunction with boxing combinations. Throwing punches to your opponent's head will cause him to raise his hands in defence, thus exposing his stomach so that you can strike with your front knee.

⇘**Flying knee**

Promoters pay a bonus fee to any boxer who wins by a knockout using this classic Muay Thai technique. There are two ways to deliver a jumping knee. In the modern style of Muay Thai, step with your front leg and then spring into the air using the full momentum of the spring to drive your rear knee upward under your opponent's chin. In traditional Muay Thai, step with the front leg, jump raising the rear leg as if to knee your opponent, then suddenly switch and use your front leg to deliver the knee strike.

⇦**Side knee**

Step in close to your opponent at the same time grabbing one side of his neck with either one or both of your hands. When using your left knee, use your left arm and vice versa for the right side. Throw a knee in a circular movement to the side of your opponent's body, aiming for his floating rib.

Practice makes perfect

The way to become proficient with knee techniques is by practising them on a leather kick bag because the weight of the bag will make your arms and legs very strong. The knee strike must be delivered at the same point of the bag over and over again in order to improve your coordination. A boxer should do between 50 and 100 respective straight and side-knee strikes daily. As with all Muay Thai techniques, pad work is an essential aspect of training. On the pad the boxer is learning not only how to deliver the knee strike but also how to turn and unbalance his opponent.

One of the advantages of using the knee to strike is that it can be swiftly changed into a kick if the opponent moves out of range or jumps away from the knee. For instance, the straight-knee strike can be pushed out into a front kick and the side-knee strike can be converted into a round kick. As with the elbow, the knee is mainly a short-range weapon with the practitioner needing skill to get within range to defuse the threat of an opponent's kicks and punches. One impressive method of getting in close to an opponent is to use a flying knee technique that can achieve one of the most spectacular knockouts in Muay Thai and, even if missed, lands the boxer very close to his opponent where he is able to execute clinches and knee techniques.

The boxer does not have to lock the opponent's neck or body to deliver a knee technique. It can be implemented from a standing position without holding the opponent. One example that is quite common in the Muay Thai ring is where a boxer throws a stream of

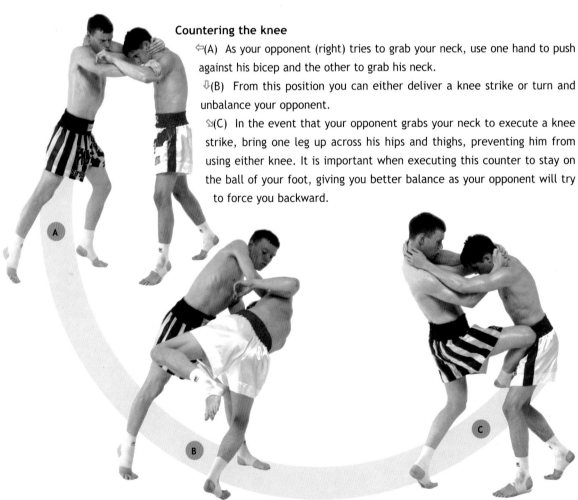

Countering the knee

⇐(A) As your opponent (right) tries to grab your neck, use one hand to push against his bicep and the other to grab his neck.

⇩(B) From this position you can either deliver a knee strike or turn and unbalance your opponent.

⬃(C) In the event that your opponent grabs your neck to execute a knee strike, bring one leg up across his hips and thighs, preventing him from using either knee. It is important when executing this counter to stay on the ball of your foot, giving you better balance as your opponent will try to force you backward.

punches at his opponent's head, causing him to raise his hands in defence. This exposes his mid-section and allows the boxer to deliver a straight knee to his opponent's solar plexus, usually culminating in a TKO.

Likewise, clinching can be used as a separate tactic to deplete an opponent's energy, namely by holding him around his waist, restricting his breathing and thus draining his energy. Alternatively, by clinching and twisting the opponent, you will cause him to fall heavily crashing down on his back on the canvas. As a result, he will be winded, losing up to 30 per cent of his energy. These are just two examples of the effectiveness of clinch work.

It is vital when using clinch work and knee techniques to have good rhythm. It is a common sight in *Muay Thai* camps to see the boxing ring filled with boxers holding the top rope and practising the skipping rhythm in perfect synchronization. If you were to listen closely you would hear that the sound made by this exercise exactly matches the beat of your own heart. Many instructors will teach this rhythm to a boxer before he is even taught how to strike with the knee.

Strengthening exercises

For clinch work the neck must be extremely strong. To strengthen the neck, a boxer can use a strap around his head with a 5–7kg(11 lb–15 lb) weight attached, and then can slowly nod his head up and down. Most training camps in Thailand improvise and use a paint pot filled with cement for this exercise.

Good indicators of a boxer's strength in the clinch are well-developed broad lats (latissimus dorsi). An essential piece of training equipment in this regard is a chin-up bar with which a boxer should complete as many chin-ups as possible everyday. This serves to strengthen and develop the muscles of the arms and upper back. To this end, a boxer can also repeatedly strike a tyre with a heavy steel bar. This exercise is used in modern Bangkok but, in earlier times, boxers chopped logs to gain strength in their upper bodies. Another form of training, sometimes seen today, was the climbing of coconut trees to improve upper-body strength. Where no coconut trees were available, a rope with knots tied along its length was hung from the ceiling of a gym and used for the same purpose.

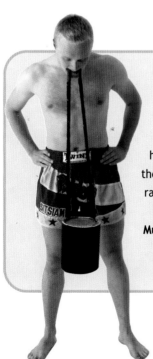

Neck strengthening exercise

A boxer grips, between his teeth, a rope attached to a dumbbell or cement-filled paint pot weighing about 1–1.5kg (2–3lb). He then raises and lowers his head slowly. By gripping the rope with his teeth, the boxer strengthens the muscles of his jaw, while raising and lowering the weight strengthens his neck.

NB: Only attempt this exercise if you are an advanced Muay Thai student and under the supervision of a teacher.

Kicks (*Daet*)

Kicks are visually the most spectacular of all the techniques of Muay Thai. They are usually the first techniques thrown when the bell sounds for the start of a match and provide an awesome demonstration, even to the uninitiated, of the tremendous power of the art. One's first visit to any Muay Thai amphitheatre provides a stunning experience of the 'Science of Eight Limbs', as the boxers kick with full power at their opponents; a shin slams into a thigh with a dull thudding sound or a foot connects with a sharp slap to an opponent's neck.

One can easily understand how the misnomer 'kickboxing' has been applied to Muay Thai; for many people what stands out most in a Thai boxing context are the large number and variety of kicks used by the boxers. Although calling Muay Thai 'kickboxing' is like waving a red rag at a bull for most Muay Thai practitioners, the name aptly describes a fighting art that has an abundance of kicking techniques.

> *In Thai culture, it is rude to point your feet toward somebody's head; therefore using the front kick to the face would be an insult.*

Front kicks (*Teep*)

⇦**Front kick to the body**

Executed with either the front or rear leg, you can use the front kick in a similar manner to a boxing jab. Using the ball of your foot and rising high on the rear leg, use this technique to either stop your opponent advancing (*see* left) or to measure the distance between you for a follow-up technique. You can also use your rear leg to attack. Rising high on the supporting leg, drive your rear leg into your opponent's body using either the ball or flat of your foot, heel or toes. The target areas can be the solar plexus, lower stomach or the chest.

⇨ **Front kick (*teep*) to the face**

Traditionally known as *Bata Loop Pak*, this technique can be executed using either the front or rear leg. Slightly bend your knees and drive your kicking leg up toward your opponent's face. Straighten both your legs at the moment of impact, using your foot in a similar manner to piercing with a spear. You can use either the ball or heel of your foot to strike under your opponent's chin, or your toes to push into his throat. To master this you would have to practise, constantly tapping the heavy bag with your toes. This is not advisable for novice students.

Generally speaking Muay Thai kicks fall into two categories: kicks using the foot to strike a target and kicks using the shin to strike a target. Kicks with the foot include the front and side kicks and kicks with the shin include the round kick.

The front kick (*teep*) is known as the 'Number One' technique in Muay Thai. This kick can be delivered using either the ball of the foot, the heel or the entire sole of the foot. By constantly pushing the opponent away with the front kick, the opponent is unable to come within striking distance. A boxer, expert in kicking, can use his legs to great advantage by keeping an opponent at bay, stopping his adversary from using a punch, knee or elbow because the distance between them is too great. Alternately, the boxer can use his kicks to attack, putting his opponent on the defensive, thus exposing other targets on which to use his shorter range weapons in boxing, knee and elbow strikes.

The most common of the kicks is the round kick (*Daet*) that uses the shin and instep to strike the

Round kicks and blocking

⇦ Low kick
The low kick can be performed with either the left or right leg and it can be delivered to your opponent's inner or outer thigh. From a left guarding position, step to your left, with your left leg at approximately 45 degrees. Rising high on your toes, twist using your left leg to pivot your body. Swing your right leg as if hitting with a staff (*Plong*), using the shin to strike. Always use your left hand to protect your chin. The opposite applies for execution of this technique from a right guarding position.

⇨ Body kick
This technique is similar to the low kick in every respect except that the target is your opponent's body. When thrown, this kick weakens him. When delivered to his arms it causes them to tire quickly, making him drop his guard and thus exposing his chin. The power generated in round kicks is achieved by the pivot on your support leg and the twist of your body using maximum rotation of your hips. To illustrate this technique, take a long stick and use it to swing and strike a punch bag as hard as you can. You will see and feel the power generated from this swinging motion.

target, There are several ways of using this kick. The low round kick is delivered with the shin and directed to the thigh, and the back or side of the knee. Next, there is the round kick to the body aimed at the floating rib or the rib cage, again delivered with the shin.

Both of these kicks can be used to weaken an opponent but can often cause an early stoppage, the low kick rendering the opponent helpless with a dead leg and the body kick winding an opponent, rendering him unable to continue. These types of stoppages don't cause any lasting damage but cause enough incapacity to enable the boxer to win the bout.

The round kick to the body can also cause an opponent to lower his arms to protect himself, thus exposing his neck and enabling the boxer to deliver his *pièce de resistance*: a high round kick with his instep directed at the opponent's neck, resulting in a knockout.

The round kick is thrown in an arcing movement. If the opponent moves out of range and the kick misses the intended target, it seems delivering the kick this way exposes the side or back of the boxer's body. In fact his body is never exposed because if the boxer finishes the move with his side or back toward the opponent, he can quickly deliver a side or back kick.

For kicking, the shin has to be extremely hard. Thai boxers get their shins hard by training on a rigid surface and by constantly kicking a heavy leather kick bag. As with all Muay Thai techniques, pad work is essential. The trainer wears the abdominal protector and shin guards, and holds the long mitts, becoming a moving target representing the opponent. By using the front kick to the abdominal protector, the boxer constantly

⬈High round kick
A high round kick can be delivered forcefully with your shin or instep to either the neck or side of your opponent's jaw, and can cause a spectacular knockout.

Legs contain the largest muscles in the body and take the most energy to move, so it is essential to increase your overall stamina and endurance by jogging.

⬆Jumping round kick
A jumping round kick is delivered with the same aim to either the head, neck or body of your opponent, using your shin to strike.

keeps the trainer at the precise distance to deliver his long-range weapons with power and accuracy. The pad-man can quickly move pads to represent different target areas while still being able to counterattack with round kicks that the boxer blocks with his shins.

It is important for a boxer to practise shadow boxing using a mirror so that he can check his guard and the positioning of his kicks. Kicking through with every technique in shadow boxing teaches the boxer balance. Shadow boxing in this way also increases his speed.

Counter kicks

↗ Spinning kick

The origins of this technique are outlined in Chapter 6 (*see* p68). This is one of the techniques which best illustrates the beauty of *Silapa Muay Thai*: the art of Muay Thai. To perform this technique from a left guarding position, step with your left leg across to the right (Number 3 in the *Yang Sarm Khum* movement). Lift your elbows slightly to gain maximum spin. Rise up on the ball of your left foot and spin your body around quickly; throw your right leg in a whipping motion with your knee slightly bent. Straightening your leg just before impact, strike either with your heel to your opponent's neck (*see* right) or the flat of your foot to his jaw. This can result in a spectacular knockout and is one of the techniques that promoters will pay a high bonus fee to see.

↘ Counter high kick with *teep*

When an opponent (right) attempts a high kick, *teep* his body to cause him to lose balance. If he kicks with his right leg, *teep* with your right leg, and vice versa.

⇐ Counter body kick with low kick

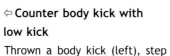

Thrown a body kick (left), step to the side in the *Yang Sarm Khum* movement; use a low round kick aiming for your opponent's Achilles tendon and sweep him to the floor.

Defence techniques

It is said that Muay Thai does not have any defensive techniques. This can seem ambiguous as boxers use forearms, elbows and shins to block. Parrying and evasion are also part of the Muay Thai repertoire. What this does infer is that in Muay Thai it is always safer to evade a technique than to counterattack it. This causes no damage to yourself and will result in your opponent finishing in a vulnerable or exposed position. Should you, nevertheless, choose to use your elbows and knees in a clinch, you will need to have a very strong defence. In this situation, you will need to move forward toward your opponent, defending yourself from a barrage of kicks and punches, before you are able to reach your preferred fighting distance. Outlined in this section are ssome of these defensive tactics.

⇩Cross block

When your opponent throws a kick, come up high on your toes (right), blocking across. Your right leg blocks a right kick and vice versa with your left leg.

⬀Blow low kick

To block the low round kick, come up high on your toes (right), blocking the kick with your upper shin.

⇦Block body kick

A block body kick is similar to a low kick block, but you must raise your knee higher so that your knee and elbow touch, creating a wall of bone.

⇩Defence against *teep*

When your opponent (right) throws a *teep*, slip your body to the side and away from the kick, at the same time catching his ankle. As an alternate defence, the *teep* can be parried.

⇨Ducking from high kick

When your opponent throws a high round kick, duck below the kick. This can cause him to lose balance. He will also find himself in an exposed position with his back turned, leaving him vulnerable to your attack.

⇧Grab leg from body kick

When your opponent round kicks to your body, side step away catching his leg and gripping it strongly. It is important to protect your chin with your other hand.

⇨Grab knee and turn

In the clinch when your opponent throws a side knee strike, quickly grab him under the thigh with one hand while your other hand goes across to grab his neck. Pull with the hand holding his neck and at the same time raise the arm holding the leg, putting your opponent off balance.

⇦Clinch and lock

When your opponent (right) clinches, grab him around the waist, sliding both your feet backward, squeezing him tightly and pressing your chin into the nerve below his collarbone. This brings him down to the floor. This technique is known as 'Giant Steals the Girl'. It is not permitted nowadays to grab the lower back, as this technique can cause back injuries.

⇨Turning from the back

When your opponent (right) clinches, quickly grab him around the waist, then step with your right leg behind his left leg, pulling him backward over your knee, causing him to fall heavily.

TRADITIONAL TECHNIQUES

Muay Thai has a rich cultural heritage. It can be likened to a beautiful tapestry interwoven with the multi-faceted culture, religious beliefs, myths and legends of the fascinating kingdom of Thailand.

There are said to be more than 40 techniques known as *Mae Mai* (master tricks) and *Luk Mai* (complementary tricks) in Muay Thai. Formulated by ancient Muay Thai masters and passed on by word of mouth from father to son, and teacher to student over many generations these are techniques and tricks by which a boxer may claim certain victory.

The master tricks of Muay Thai are winning techniques that can result in a spectacular knockout or an injury so serious that it renders an opponent unable to continue. The complementary tricks, on the other hand, are as the name implies, supplementary techniques that are added to a boxer's complement of tricks and tactics. These techniques are designed to achieve several things with regard to an opponent: unbalance and weaken him, cause minor injuries or cause him to lose concentration.

There may be slight differences in the classification of complementary and master techniques. This may occur when the use of a complementary technique has resulted in immediate victory for a boxer, in which case the teacher would reclassify it in the master category. An example of this is the *Hanuman Hak Kor Erawan*. When executing this technique the boxer pulls the opponent's head down sharply and then delivers a knee strike to the body; the classification for this technique would be in the complementary category, however were the knee to be delivered to the opponent's face resulting in a knockout (*see* p67), the classification then becomes a master technique.

All teachers will know at least 15 master tricks and 15 complementary tricks, but may know more or even different variations according to regional influences.

The warrior's stance in the traditional martial arts of Thailand was longer and lower, similar to a kung fu or karate stance. This was to give a firm base for better balance when fighting on the battlefield or on uneven ground. A boxer could take advantage of this low stance by stepping on the upper thighs of his opponent to deliver a dramatic technique such as a round kick, a side knee or downward elbow strike to the opponent's head. Many of these techniques require supreme athletic skills and gymnastic abilities, but several of them are considered to be too dangerous for use in the modern sport of Muay Thai. Today this traditional style of fighting, known as *Muay Kaacheurk* (fighting with bound fists), is choreographed into spectacular demonstrations performed at cultural fairs and festivals.

Interest in the traditional techniques declined in favour of the modern ring sport, until recent years. Many camps and schools did not teach this method of fighting because training time was needed to prepare the boxers for competition, but as the sport of Muay Thai grew in popularity worldwide, many foreign students became interested in the history and development of the art.

The vast majority of the traditional techniques relate to stories from the *Ramakien*, which was adapted around AD600 from the 2000-year-old original. In it, Lord Rama, Vishnu's incarnation on earth and heir to the throne of Ayodhaya, the legendary kingdom in Northern India, is banished from heaven and spends 14 years in exile on earth with his wife Sita and his

opposite THE OLD STYLE OF MUAY THAI HAD A LONG STANCE, AND BECAUSE OF THIS, THE BOXER COULD GAIN THE ADVANTAGE BY STEPPING ON HIS OPPONENT'S FRONT LEG AND DELIVERING A POWERFUL KICK TO HIS HEAD OR NECK.

brother Lakshman. With the assistance of the monkey army commander, Hanuman, they set out to destroy the forces of evil on earth.

This thrilling story contains romance, adventure, heroism, martial arts, magic, demons and gods. Some of the characters with martial art connections are Rama, who is Vishnu's resident in the cosmic ocean until reborn on earth to destroy evil demons; Erawan, the god Indra's white, three-headed elephant steed; Naga, the mighty serpent king, and Hanuman, the

HANUMAN TAWAI WEN — THIS TECHNIQUE DEPICTS THE MONKEY GOD HANUMAN PRESENTING THE RING TO SITA. THE TECHNIQUE IS DELIVERED WITH BOTH FISTS, BUT IF THE HANDS WERE BOUND WITH ROPE, THE FISTS WOULD SKIM THE SURFACE OF THE OPPONENT'S SKIN, CAUSING LACERATIONS TO HIS FACE.

monkey god, with white fur that sparkles like diamonds — Rama's greatest warrior.

Hanuman is an icon to all Thai boxers who wish to emulate his courage, fortitude and exceptional martial skills. Many boxers carry a picture of Hanuman complete with sacred *Khom* script, which is worn inside the *Kruang Ruang* or Pra Jer to bring good luck during a bout. Some may even have a tattoo of Hanuman on their left bicep. In olden times Hanuman tattoos were done using the blood of a monkey in the belief that the spirit of Hanuman would possess the boxer's body. Many older teachers say that in ancient times, when a boxer with such a tattoo performed the *Wai Kru/Ram Muay*, he would go into a trance, taking on the features and mannerisms of the monkey god. The boxer who truly believed himself possessed by the spirit of Hanuman would see himself as invincible and indestructible, and therefore assured of certain victory.

It is thought that some traditional Muay Thai techniques are related to stories from the Ramakien for use as a teaching aid, making it easier for boxers to memorize them. Some examples of these are as follows:

Hanuman Tawai Wen
Rama's wife Sita is abducted by the demon king, Tosakanth, and taken to the evil kingdom of Longka. Rama enlists Hanuman's aid in rescuing his beloved queen, sending him to Longka with Sita's ring in order to prove his identity. This was so that Sita would trust him and come back with Hanuman to Ayodhaya. This technique (*see* opposite) depicts Hanuman offering the ring to Sita.

Hanuman Hak Kor Erawan
During the wars between Longka and Ayodhaya, Tosakanth summoned his favourite son, Indrachit, to lead his troops. Indrachit transformed himself into the Lord Indra, seated on Erawan, his white elephant steed, and entered the battlefield in this disguise. Lakshman, who was leading the Ayodhayan army, believed this to be Indra and called off his monkey troops, whereupon Indrachit unleashed a magic arrow rendering everybody but Hanuman immobile either

critically injured or unconscious. Hanuman realized that this was not the Lord Indra. Seeing through the evil Indrachit's disguise, he mounted the elephant, killing it. This technique therefore depicts Hanuman swooping down from the sky to break the false Erawan's neck.

Pra Rama Nao Sorn
This technique is from the story of the Lord Rama hunting the golden deer, and depicts him drawing back the bow to fire a golden arrow.

As explained earlier, some of these techniques may have different interpretations. *Hanuman Hak Kor Erawan,* for instance, can be performed in any of the following ways:

■ When the opponent comes in to clinch, the boxer grabs the top of his head with two hands pulling it down sharply to deliver a straight knee up to his opponent's face.

■ When the opponent comes in to clinch, the boxer will grab with both hands on the side of the head, pulling him down to deliver a straight-knee strike.

■ When the opponent comes in to clinch, the boxer will grab him around the neck, pulling him into a head lock, leaning back and applying pressure to his neck. The boxer will then deliver a powerful knee strike to the opponent's body.

■ Another variation is when a boxer delivers a flying knee strike under his opponent's chin while delivering a downward elbow strike to the top of his head.

Mae Mai Muay Thai
Mae Mai Muay Thai techniques show supreme mastery of the art of Muay Thai. Many of these techniques are, however, obsolete today and are more for use in warfare or self-defence.

Hak Kor Mahingsa
When an opponent throws a punch, the boxer slips to the side so that the punch goes over his shoulder. The boxer's arm then goes around the opponent's neck trapping his arm. Thereafter, the boxer delivers a knee strike to the opponent's solar plexus.

CHORAKED FAAD HANG (CROCODILE WHIPS HIS TAIL) — THIS TECHNIQUE CALLS FOR GOOD FLEXIBILITY AND SPEED. OLD MASTERS IN ALL MARTIAL ARTS OFTEN STUDIED THE INSTINCTIVE DEFENSIVE MOVEMENTS OF BIRDS AND ANIMALS. THE CROCODILE WOULD HAVE BEEN ONE SUCH CREATURE, WHIPPING ITS TAIL TO KNOCK ITS PREY OFF BALANCE. THE EXECUTION OF THIS TECHNIQUE CALLS FOR GOOD FLEXIBILITY AND SPEED.

that impacts with the rib cage, or to the back to strike the kidney area.

Pra Rama Yieb Longka

The boxer suddenly springs into the air above his opponent, with one foot landing on the opponent's thigh and the other landing on his shoulder. The boxer then delivers a downward elbow strike to the top of the opponent's head.

Tad Mala

A straight uppercut elbow under the chin, this technique is delivered to counter whatever attack an opponent wishes to use. The boxer moves in swiftly, getting very close to his opponent, causing his elbow to ride off his opponent's chest, striking under his chin.

Hak Nguang Iyara

When the opponent kicks with a round kick, the boxer grabs this leg scooping the kick under his arm and delivering a powerful downward strike elbow to his opponent's upper thigh.

Hanuman Tawai Wen

This is a double uppercut punch. In the modern sport this technique is delivered to the opponent's chin resulting in a knockout, but in the traditional technique the fists slide upward across the opponent's face with the hemp-bound hands used to cut and lacerate it.

Java Saad Hok

This technique has two variations: when the opponent throws a punch, the boxer lowers his body to the side and then delivers either an elbow strike to the front

Mon Yan Lak

Before an opponent's round kick strikes the boxer, he uses a front kick to the opponent's chest. This sends him off-balance and crashing to the floor.

Hanuman Hern Weha

The boxer jumps into the air, stepping onto the opponent's thigh and delivering a powerful round-knee strike to the side of his opponent's head.

Pra Narai Kham Samut

The boxer springs into the air, stepping onto his opponent's thigh, and delivers a round kick to his head.

Choraked Faad Hang

A spinning kick: when the boxer attacks with a high round kick and the opponent leans away to avoid this attack, the boxer quickly spins his body to strike his opponent's temple or nape of his neck with his heel.

Hak Kor Erawan

When an opponent comes in to clinch, the boxer grabs his head, pulling it down sharply to deliver a straight knee strike up to his opponent's face.

Naga Bidt Haang

When an opponent front kicks, the boxer grabs his foot by the heel and toes. Twisting the foot, he delivers a knee strike to his opponent's hamstring.

HANUMAN HAK DAAN — TO PERFORM THIS TECHNIQUE THE BOXER MUST BE LIGHTNING FAST AND DELIVER A KNEE AND ELBOW STRIKE SIMULTANEOUSLY TO COUNTER THE OPPONENT'S STRAIGHT PUNCH.

HAK KOR ERAWAN (BREAKING THE ELEPHANT'S NECK) — THIS TECHNIQUE CAN STILL BE SEEN IN PROFESSIONAL MUAY THAI BOUTS WORLDWIDE. IT IS DANGEROUS AND CAN RESULT IN A CLEAN KNOCKOUT.

These techniques require supreme skills and athletic ability and should never be attempted unless under proper supervision.

KORN HANUMAN TAI YAN IS ONE OF THE RARE MASTER TECHNIQUES OF MUAY THAI. IT REQUIRES GREAT AGILITY AS THE BOXER MUST SPRING RAPIDLY INTO THE AIR, STRIKING UNDER HIS OPPONENT'S CHIN WITH HIS KNEE.

HANUMAN KRUK FUN

This is one of the traditional techniques which have been outlawed in the modern sport. In it the opponent (left) clinches the boxer's neck (A), who suddenly drops to the floor delivering a straight upward kick with the ball of his foot to the opponent's groin (B), a foul blow which is what has made this technique obsolete in the modern sport.

Pak Taitoy

When an opponent throws a punch, the boxer steps past it, delivering a backward elbow strike to the rear of his opponent's head.

Dab Chawala

This is a sharp straight punch delivered to the eyeball.

Hanuman Hak Daan

When an opponent throws a punch, the boxer quickly side-steps simultaneously delivering a side elbow strike to the side of his opponent's jaw as well as a round knee strike to his solar plexus.

Luk Mai Muay Thai

Luk Mai Muay Thai, as in the case of *Mae Mai Muay Thai* techniques, were part of a compulsory syllabus in many Muay Thai camps in former times. A boxer would be expected to learn and perfect a minimum of 15 master and 15 complementary tricks as an essential part of his study of the art. In olden times these techniques were not taught to foreign students as they were considered a warfare secret.

Khun Yak Pa Nang

When an opponent grabs a boxer's neck with the intention to clinch, the boxer quickly grabs his opponent around the waist, and gripping his own forearms, bends his opponent over backward. This technique is not permitted in modern Muay Thai due to the damage this can cause the lower back. However, boxers are permitted to do the same manoeuvre with the arms positioned higher up the body.

⇨ Mai Ya Lab Lak Pra

Although this technique is not illegal in the modern-day ring it is never seen because of its complexity. The boxer drops down and, while his opponent's kick is in mid-flight, pulls his adversary's lower leg and pushes the inner thigh, bringing him crashing down sideways on to the floor. This technique can cause serious injury.

Erawan Soi Naga

This is a long uppercut strike with the fist thrown to an opponent's chin. The technique can be used when an opponent performs a round kick, with the boxer quickly stepping inside the kick to deliver a long uppercut to the opponent's chin. It can also be used in the same manner to counter a punch attack.

Bata Loop Pak

This is a front kick to an opponent's face. This can be considered very insulting to a Thai contestant as, in Thai culture, it is rude to show the soles of one's feet to another and the head is considered sacred.

Hiran Muan Pandin

When an opponent performs a round kick, the boxer steps across, blocking with his forearm or elbow to the

opponent's leg, and then delivers a spinning or reverse elbow strike to his opponent's head or face. It is important when using this technique that the boxer's back rests against the opponent's body.

Tain Kwadlan

When an opponent executes a round kick to the body or head, the boxer steps across and with a very low kick, the toe just gliding across the floor, the boxer's lower shin connects to the opponent's Achilles tendon, sweeping him to the ground.

Kwang Liew Lang

When a boxer delivers a round kick to his opponent's body, and the opponent moves to avoid it, the boxer quickly turns and delivers a back kick to his mid-section or up under his chin with the sole or heel of his foot.

Pra Rama Sakod Tab

This is a very dangerous technique as the front kick is delivered with the toes, pointed in a stabbing or piercing motion, to the opponent's throat. In olden times boxers would kick a hard surface with their toes to strengthen them for the execution of this technique.

Tayae Kamsao

This is a very subtle technique. When an opponent throws a round kick to the head or body, the boxer front kicks his opponent's support leg just above the knee, causing him to fall down.

Koompan Poong Hok

This is an excellent counter to the Cobra punch. When an opponent

throws it, his whole body leans forward with his full weight behind the technique. The boxer simply side-steps the punch, throwing a straight knee strike up to his opponent's body.

Pra Rama Nao Sorn

When an opponent attacks with a double elbow strike to the head, the boxer blocks it by raising his forearm and delivering an uppercut punch to his solar plexus.

REUK NEUNG ERAWAN — FROM THE OPPONENT'S ROUND KICK THE BOXER SIDE-STEPS AND GRASPS THE KICKING LEG IN A STRONG GRIP, THEN DELIVERS A STRAIGHT PUNCH TO THE OPPONENT'S CHIN, RESULTING IN A KNOCKOUT. THIS IS ONE OF THE TECHNIQUES THAT HAS MADE THE TRANSITION WELL INTO THE MODERN SPORT.

Fan Look Buab

When an opponent throws a punch, the boxer steps through quickly and uses a succession of left and right side elbow strikes to cut the opponent.

Reuk Neung Erawan

When an opponent attacks with a round kick, the boxer quickly scoops the adversary's kicking leg under his arm and delivers a straight punch to the jaw. Although this is a traditional technique it is one of a few that can be seen regularly at many competitions.

Hanuman Jong Thanon

When an opponent throws a punch, the boxer side-steps to the outside, delivering a round kick, striking with the full shin to the opponent's mid-section.

Hong Peak Hag

When an opponent throws a punch, the boxer blocks the punch with his forearm and delivers either a side strike, a downward strike or an uppercut elbow to his opponent's upper arm.

Sak Puang Malai

When an opponent punches, the boxer steps through to block it with his forearm, and spins around to strike with a reverse elbow strike to his temple.

Today Muay Thai is fought in a boxing ring with an even surface, thus boxers have an upright stance that enables great speed and mobility. This stance makes some of the traditional techniques obsolete in the practice of the modern sport but many have been adapted for use by today's professional boxers; thus the authenticity of the art has been retained.

Gorn Ling Preel

This technique is very dangerous, and therefore rarely seen in the stadiums of Bangkok, but when it is performed, the boxer is greeted with rapturous applause from the audience and earns a generous bonus from the promoter.

When an opponent (right) throws a high kick, the boxer squats low, keeping his heels raised and his eyes on him (A). As the kicking leg passes over his head, and lands on the floor, the boxer quickly springs from the squat position and delivers a knee strike to the opponent's spine or shoulder blade (B).

SELF-DEFENCE

The Oxford English Dictionary defines the meaning of the word 'martial' to be 'ready, eager to fight' and the word 'art' to be 'skill, cunning, stratagem, subject in which skill may be exercised'. To summarize, 'martial art' means 'the skill of combat'.

There are many reasons why people enrol at martial arts schools but the majority will join to learn to protect themselves. Many martial arts have gravitated toward a more sport- or competition oriented syllabus but will still teach students the basic principles of self-defence. Sports martial arts and self-defence are, however, two totally different forms of combat. In competition, students are competing in a controlled environment where everybody behaves in a sportsman-like manner. The venue is well lit with a matted area or ring, there are judges and referees, and the fight must adhere to the strict rules and regulations of the sport. Students know when and where the contest will take place, and may even have some foreknowledge of their opponents' method of fighting.

In self-defence this situation is totally reversed. The attackers have the upper hand in every way. They know when, where and how they are going to attack you. In fact, the attack will definitely happen when and where you least expect it. They are no more than bullies or cowards because they always victimize somebody whom they believe to be weak.

One thing that they will have is confidence. They may 'talk' a good fight and emanate a cocky persona. They will use abusive language and name-calling to degrade you, making you feel small, simply to help build up their own confidence for an attack. In the art of Krabi Krabong, *Fan Daab* sword fighting, this verbal abuse is what is known as 'unnecessary movement': somebody 'spinning a sword' may look impressive but it doesn't achieve anything. This is just one form of attack: there is of course, the ambush: when the attacker strikes you unawares. In this situation, attackers use the element of surprise to their advantage, giving the victim very little opportunity to react.

The first principle of good self-defence is common sense. In addition, training in martial arts also helps a person stay focused and able to make decisions in a split second. It teaches self-control and self-discipline. These are major advantages to knowing self-defence. Training in martial arts fine-tunes your skill of discernment and gives you an added advantage of being able to remain calm and make a rational choice. The worst scenario is one in which you have no other alternative but to defend yourself, with your fighting technique being the only factor ensuring your survival.

Muay Thai is a full contact sport, and its fighting techniques are powerful, designed to cause maximum damage. In a competition, a kick to the leg can disable

Some ground rules to remember:

- Don't walk down quiet, dark streets alone
- Stay in well-lit areas
- Don't accept lifts from strangers
- Don't take shortcuts across fields or down alleyways
- Ensure you lock your car doors when stopping at traffic lights and keep the windows closed
- Use registered or government taxis with drivers' details and licence numbers on display.
- A mobile phone can be a great asset, so ensure your battery is charged and that you have sufficient credit to call a friend to collect you if a situation looks dangerous.

opposite AN ATTACK CAN HAPPEN ANYWHERE AND AT ANY TIME SO ALWAYS BE VIGILANT.

a boxer just enough to gain victory. In self-defence this technique gives a victim time to decide her next course of action. The elbows can cut like swords, scarring an adversary, making it easier for police to identify an attacker. A punch can cause a clean knockout or can be delivered to the body to disable an assailant. The knee, in turn, can be used at close quarters and delivered to the groin, the body or the head. The basic principles and techniques of Muay Thai are enough to enable people to defend themselves. They must be constantly practised to make them an instinctive reaction.

Legal implications in self-defence

Always remember that Muay Thai's techniques are dangerous and designed to cause maximum damage. It's essential that you use the minimum force necessary to enable you to escape from your attacker. You should never follow up with an attack after an assailant is incapacitated. This could leave you open to legal action as you might then be considered the aggressor.

The laws with regard to self-defence vary from country to country. In England, for instance, it is legal to defend yourself by using equal force as exerted by your attacker; for example, if an attacker punches you, you can punch back with equal force. You cannot kick or use a weapon against him. This would be considered illegal and unnecessary force and could see you in court charged with assault.

The decision to defend yourself is a difficult one, compounded by the fact that you only have split seconds to decide what is legal in the situation you find yourself. A golden rule is to do only what is necessary to allow you to get away safely from an assailant. You should then report the incident to a relevant law-enforcement agency at the earliest opportunity. In this way, you ensure your safety and, to the best of your knowledge and ability, you have acted within the law. Most importantly, the authorities are aware of it and able to take follow-up action to prevent a recurrence.

Attack with a weapon

⇧(A) The assailant lunges forward with a knife. The girl side-steps, gripping the assailant's arm with two hands.

⇧(B) She delivers a knee strike to his elbow joint, disabling the hand with the knife.

⇧(C) The girl follows up with a side kick to the assailant's knee joint, temporarily disabling him and allowing her time to get away.

Defence against a swinging punch

⇦(A) The assailant throws a swinging punch at the girl. She blocks his arm with her forearm.

⇨(B) At the same time she delivers an elbow to the opponent's face.

⇦(C) From the elbow she grips the back of the assailant's neck.

⇨(D) Stepping back, she jerks the assailant's head forward.

⇦(E) She pulls the assailant's head down into a more vulnerable position.

⇨(F) And follows up by delivering a straight upward knee strike to the opponent's face.

TRAINING IN THAILAND

Recent years have seen a noticeable trend of foreign boxers making a pilgrimage to Thailand that is, in effect, a rite of passage marking their coming of age in the world of Muay Thai. To accommodate the overseas students, many owners of Muay Thai camps have extended their curriculum.

Often, foreign students tend to think they can just pack up their backpacks and go. It's not that easy and training in Thailand needs preparation and careful planning. Factors that need to be considered are duration of stay in Thailand, visa requirements, health considerations and budgetary constraints.

It is essential that students consult their doctor or local health authority before leaving their country of residence. When travelling to Thailand, particularly if training in provincial camps, visiting students must have the necessary vaccinations. These usually include typhoid, cholera, hepatitis B, polio and tetanus. Students should check with their doctor for up-to-date information on immunization. It's advisable to take a basic first-aid kit. In Bangkok and main tourist areas, all pharmacists speak English so it's easy to explain any health problems and to obtain correct treatment, but in the provinces this may be more difficult.

Visiting students should ensure they have the necessary training kit, which consists of shorts, bag gloves and skipping ropes. All camps will have these items for general use but remember: most Thai people are a lot smaller than foreigners so it's advisable to take your own equipment.

Arriving at the camp

Students shouldn't just arrive at a camp unannounced, expecting training and accommodation to be organized for them there and then. There may only be room at the camp for the resident boxers. Before leaving for Thailand, foreign students would be well advised to write to the camp to let them know they are coming. Remember that living conditions in the camp will be very basic. It is more advisable, therefore, to find a hotel or guesthouse close to the camp that can be used as a base.

There are two training sessions daily at every camp. The first begins at 06:30 and ends at 08:30 and the later session runs from 15:00 until 17:00. These are ideal times for training in this climate as it is cooler early in the morning and in the late afternoon. Remember, even then, the temperature will be around 30°C(86°F) so visiting students should take their own bottled water. If foreigners wish to train and fight in Thailand, they will be expected to train at all sessions but if they are there only to further their

above BOXERS HAVE THE OPPORTUNITY TO TRAIN WITH ARJARN SENNANAN AT SITYODTONG CAMP IN THAILAND.

opposite THE GRAND PALACE IS A MAJOR TOURIST ATTRACTION IN THAILAND, PARTICULARLY ON 5 DECEMBER EACH YEAR WHEN THAIS CELEBRATE HIS MAJESTY THE KING OF THAILAND'S BIRTHDAY THERE.

studies, they will be able to choose a session suited to their schedules. Many new schools will have standard weekly or monthly fees for training and accommodation at the camp.

Thailand is deservedly called 'The Land of Smiles' and students will find everybody at the camp extremely friendly. Foreign students should be accustomed to the etiquette of Muay Thai, namely that of bowing (wai) to all instructors and seniors. It would be appropriate when arriving at the camp to bow to the owner and the head teacher, but it would be considered rather strange if you were to bow to everybody at the school. The reasoning for the wai is very complex and it is not just a way of saying 'hello' or 'goodbye'. In fact, most Thai people would not expect a foreigner to bow: a simple 'hello' and a smile would be perfectly acceptable. However, it would be deemed appropriate to follow up a 'thank you' with a bow after a trainer has taken you through your paces on the pads. To a Thai teacher, being courteous and polite shows the moral strength of a student, and is considered to be a valuable asset in a boxer.

It's appropriate when training at a Muay Thai camp in Thailand that you always check with the *Arjarn* before doing anything. You might, for instance, wish to give a gift to one of the boxers, but there exists a strict hierarchy. Although your intentions are basically well meant, besides possibly offending somebody at the camp you could also embarass the boxer himself. You should always give any gifts directly to the Arjarn who will then distribute these to the boxers accordingly.

By training in Thailand you'll learn to appreciate why Muay Thai is a superior fighting art. The boxers are true devotees, dedicating their lives to Muay Thai. Rising at 06:00, the day begins with a 5—8km(3—5mi) run, then back to the camp for bag work, pad work, skipping and shadow boxing for 5 x 3-minute rounds respectively. Some camps even do 5 x 5-minute rounds of each exercise. The next session is from 15:00 to 17:00 following the same arduous routine as the dawn session. The evenings are then spent either going to stadiums to watch one of the boxers fight or watching Muay Thai on television. The boxers live, eat and sleep Muay Thai.

Important points of etiquette

- Do not point your feet at people, religious objects or shrines.
- Do not point with your finger.
- Do not stride over somebody who is seated.
- Do not touch a person's head or pass anything over their head. This is because the head is considered sacred in Thai culture.
- Do not lose your temper; this shows a lack of control.
- Do not shout or act in a boisterous manner.
- Do not remove your shirt in public.
- Many years ago, visitors to Rajadamnern Stadium were required to wear semi-formal clothing. Nowadays, many foreign students turn up for fights wearing no more than shorts and vests. Being a student of Muay Thai you should always show respect by wearing trousers and a shirt when visiting stadiums.
- Always wear trousers, a shirt with sleeves and full shoes (not sandals) when visiting palaces or government-owned buildings.
- Always remove your shoes when entering temples or people's homes.
- The Thai royal family is highly respected by Thai people. Never make any derogatory remarks about them and treat any images of the king and queen, as well as those of the royal family with the utmost respect.

By following this advice, students will show an understanding of the customs, etiquette and traditions of Thailand and gain social acceptance in Muay Thai circles.

opposite IN CAMPS BOXERS PRACTISE THEIR TECHNIQUES FOR 5 X 3 MINUTES OR 5 X 5 MINUTES ON PADS OR BAGS. HERE A BOXER IS BEING PUT THROUGH HIS PACES PRACTISING THE LOW ROUND KICK.

Muay Thai for Sport

Muay Thai, Thailand's national sport, enjoys immense popularity throughout the country, so much so that it is televised daily with thousands of Thais avidly viewing the broadcasts.

Live Muay Thai contests take place at either the Rajadamnern or Lumpini stadiums every day of the week. Muay Thai bouts are also held every Sunday afternoon on the premises of Channel 7 television, the studio of which is transformed into a Muay Thai stadium for the day. Muay Thai tournaments are also staged at least one night a week in every small town and province across the kingdom, and bouts are very popular at many of Thailand's festivals and fetes where local boxers have the opportunity to display their talents in front of a local crowd.

One of the biggest events in the Muay Thai calendar is in honour of His Majesty the King of Thailand's birthday. This spectacular tournament is free to the public and takes place every year on 5 December at Sanam Luang, the great common in front of the Grand Palace in Bangkok. This tournament has become a major tourist attraction for many foreigners wishing to see boxers from all over the world participating in this prestigious competition.

The professional sport of Muay Thai has seen a steady growth around the world since the early 1970s. Many countries outside Thailand, especially in Europe, now hold regular competitions: on average one a month. Besides the large number of people participating, the sport's live events also enjoy many spectators. Television companies have been quick to recognize the popularity of the sport and major events can now be seen regularly on television across Europe.

Since its inception in 1986, and the founding of the Amateur Muay Thai Association of Thailand (AMTAT), amateur Muay Thai has also grown in popularity and has been an official event at the Southeast Asian games for a number of years now. As with the professional sport, the amateur system has engendered great interest outside of Thailand, with many countries' sports governing bodies granting the sport official recognition. With so many Muay Thai enthusiasts worldwide it is hoped that amateur Muay Thai will soon gain the recognition it deserves as an Olympic sport.

Rules and regulations

Rules and regulations define a sport and every sport must have officials who oversee the rules and technical standards. In Muay Thai the judges and referees play an essential role in the sport and their position can be summarized as the 'keepers' of the art. In other words, they are responsible for the art's technical and administrative support.

Judges and referees work within a governing body and hold a position of equal importance to that of the sport's teachers and coaches. They have the same objectives, namely to ensure the safety of the boxers, to make sure that all the rituals and traditions of the art are adhered to and that a high technical standard is maintained within the sport.

Judges and referees are required to be mature adults of impeccable character. They need to be fit and healthy, preferably married and have a sound education. They also are required to have undergone training in judging and refereeing Muay Thai bouts and are obliged to have been a member of the governing body for Muay Thai in their native country for at least two years.

opposite EAST MEETS WEST. A BOXER FROM THE VOS GYM IN HOLLAND COMPETES AGAINST A FIGHTER FROM THE SASIPRAPA CAMP IN THAILAND. NOWADAYS MANY BOXERS FROM THAILAND TRAVEL TO MUAY THAI COMPETITIONS WORLDWIDE.

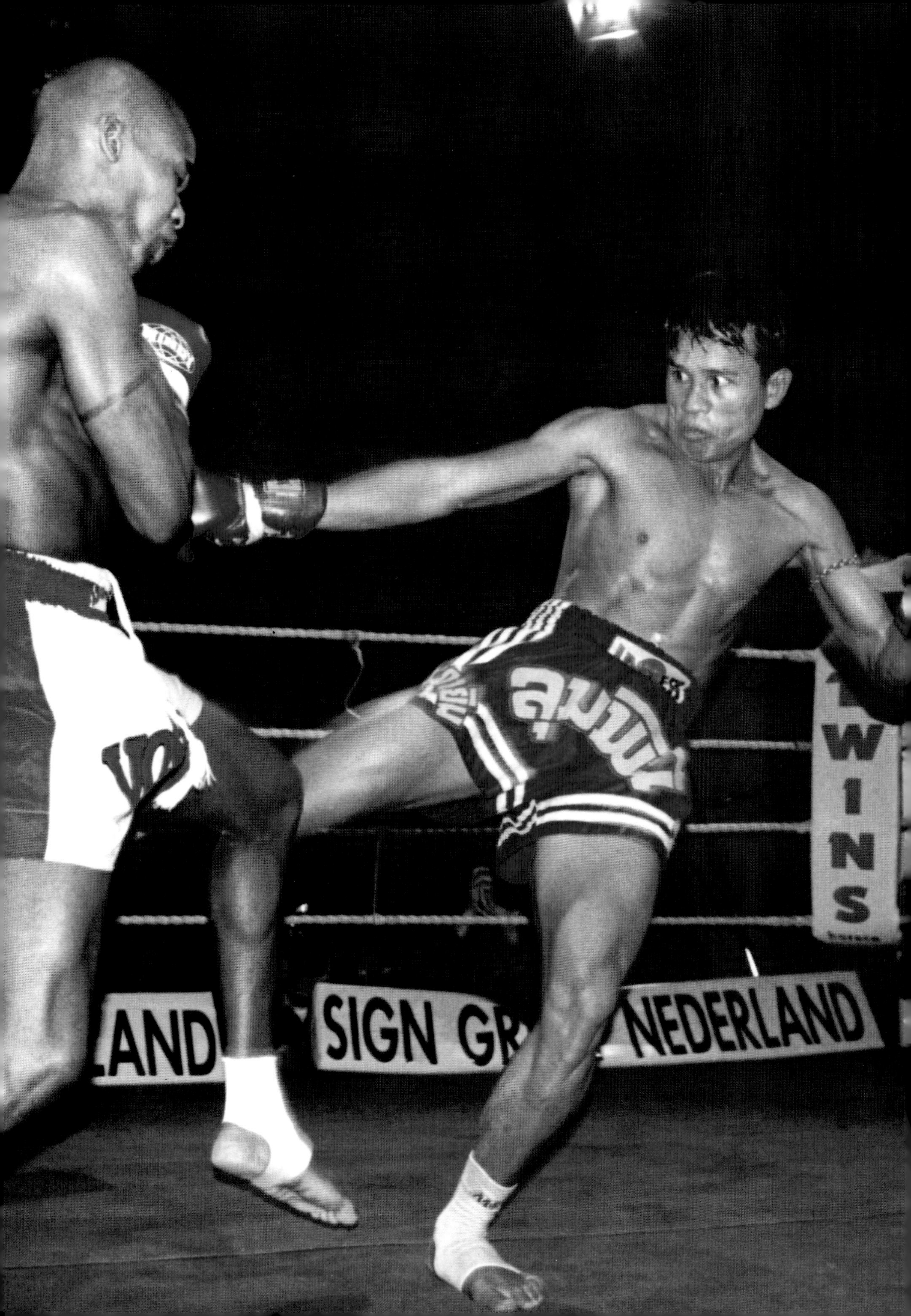
LAND
SIGN GR
NEDERLAND
WINS

Competition customs

The basic rules and regulations of the sport are constantly updated but the essence of the sport never changes:

- Every boxer must perform the *Wai Kru/Ram Muay* ritual dance before fighting.
- Music is played for the *Wai Kru/Ram Muay* and throughout the bout. Featuring the distinctive sounds of the Java flute *(Pi)*, drum *(Glawng Kaek)* and the miniature cymbals *(Ching)*, the music is played at ringsides of all stadiums throughout Thailand. A live band creates an exciting atmosphere and where there is a lull in the action, the tempo of the music picks up, encouraging the boxers to fight harder. Outside of Thailand, this music is played from a pre-recorded tape or CD, but it never really has the same authenticity as a live band.
- Full-contact bouts are fought in rounds, and points are awarded on the power and accuracy of the techniques. The judges also take into account the boxers' knowledge and mastery of Muay Thai.

The following are a condensed set of standard rules for Muay Thai bouts held throughout Europe, provided courtesy of the British Thai Boxing Council:

Promoters

- All promoters must strictly adhere to the rules and regulations. Contests must be licensed according to the local and national bylaws and regulations governing such events.

The Ring

- The ring shall be a regulation boxing ring not less than 3m²(4yd²) within the ropes. The ring floor shall be padded in a manner as approved by the governing body. Ring posts shall be properly padded.
- The ring platform shall not be more than 12m(13yd) above the floor of the building and shall be provided with suitable steps for the use of the contestants.

- The ring ropes shall be a minimum of three in number, preferably four, and not less than 3cm(1in) in diameter.
- The promoter of the event shall provide all necessary ring equipment for the use of the contestants and seconds, except for those items supplied by the contestants (*see* p86, *Contestant's equipment and seconds*, rule #1) and those items supplied by the seconds (*see* p87, *Contestant's equipment and seconds*, rule #5).
- There will be a gong or bell at the ringside which should be clear in tone so that contestants may easily hear it when sounded.

Ringside officials, personnel and duties

- A referee, a minimum of three judges, a timekeeper, a scorekeeper, a contest inspector, a master of ceremonies and a contest doctor, all sanctioned by the governing body, will be employed at all of the sanctioned events.
- All referees and judges must have completed an official Muay Thai Judges and Referees Course and must have officiated as a shadow judge until deemed by the governing body to have sufficient experience to judge and/or referee a Muay Thai contest.
- Referees and judges must be of smart appearance and wear an approved uniform. The referee should wear soft-soled shoes in the ring. The referee is not permitted to wear spectacles, jewellery (including a watch) or a waist belt. He should supply his own towel, tape and nail clippers. Officials (including the timekeeper, contest doctor and contest inspector) are not permitted to consume alcohol before or during the event.
- The timekeeper will not ring the bell to start the round until he has received the appropriate signal from the referee. The timekeeper will ring the bell to signal the start and end of each round, stopping time if required to do so by the referee. He will also keep time during the rest period. In the event of the referee giving a count at the end of the round, the timekeeper must compensate for the count before ringing the bell.
- The emcee will publicly announce the ongoing event and subsequent contests throughout the course of the proceedings in a calm, unbiased manner.

Pre-contest regulations

■ Any contestant applying for eligibility to compete in a Muay Thai contest must be examined by a qualified medical doctor prior to the day of the contest. This is to establish both physical and mental fitness for competition. A thorough physical and eye examination will be given to each contestant by the contest doctor not later than one hour before the contestant is due to enter the ring.

■ Contestants will weigh-in 24 hours prior to the bout, unless under special conditions, when the boxer will weigh-in on the day of the contest. Weigh-in is to take place in the presence of the contest inspector on scales approved by the governing body. All contestants are to be stripped to their underwear.

■ Contestants participating in a Thai boxing bout must be no less than 17 years of age.

■ All contestants must be clean and present a tidy appearance. It will be at the sole discretion of the contest inspector to determine whether contestants' facial adornments such as moustaches and beards as well as the length of the hair, present any potential hazard to their safety or their opponent's. Hair beads or hair adornments, which could cause a danger to the contestant or his opponent, are strictly prohibited. The excessive use of grease or any other foreign substance is not permitted. The referee shall have cause to remove any of these should they be in excess. Non-compliance by the contestant shall result in an immediate disqualification.

Referee's command

⇐ (1) The referee indicates the start of the action by signalling with his hand between the fighters in a downward chopping motion, at the same time speaking the word 'chok', meaning 'fight'.

↙(2) The referee says the word 'yud', meaning 'stop', before approaching the two boxers in order to separate them.

⇓ (3) The referee speaks the command 'yaek', meaning 'break' and then separates the boxers before repeating the command 'chok' to restart the bout.

Weights and classes

Junior bantamweight 50.81–52.16kg(112–115 lb)

Bantamweight 52.17–53.52kg(115–118lb)

Junior featherweight 53.53–55.34kg(118–122 lb)

Featherweight 55.35 – 57.15kg(122–126 lb)

Super featherweight 57.16–58.97kg(126–130 lb)

Lightweight 58.98–61.23kg(130–135 lb)

Super lightweight 61.24–63.50kg(135–140 lb)

Light welterweight 63.51–66.68kg(140–147 lb)

Welterweight 66.69–69.85kg(147–154 lb)

Light middleweight 69.86–72.57kg(154–160 lb)

Middleweight 72.58–75.75kg(160–167 lb)

Light heavyweight 75.76–79.38kg(167–175 lb)

Super light heavyweight 79.39–82.55kg(175–182 lb)

Cruiserweight 82.56–86.18kg(182–190 lb)

Heavyweight 86.19–95.00kg(190–209 lb)

Super heavyweight more than 95kg(209 lb)

Contestants' equipment and seconds

■ All contestants must wear Thai boxing shorts; ankle supports are optional and limited to two in total. Male contestants must wear a snug-fitting, foul-proof groin protector. Female contestants may wear a breast shield. All contestants must wear a fitted mouthpiece. No shirts, shoes or jewellery are permitted. *Kruang Ruang* (*Pra Jer*) may be wrapped around the biceps. The *Mongkon* may be worn only during the *Ram Muay* pre-fight ritual but must be removed before the start of the contest.

■ All contestants must wear the boxing gloves approved by the governing body. They should not be squeezed, kneaded or crushed to change their original shape. In bouts of welterweight or lighter, the gloves must be eight ounces each; in the light middleweight or heavier divisions the gloves must be 10 ounces each.

■ Bandages and tape should not exceed the following restrictions: soft surgical bandages not more than 51mm(2in) wide and not longer than 11m(12yd), held in place by soft material tape. Plastic or metallic tape is strictly prohibited. The placing of any item, other

than tape or bandages, inside the gloves will result in instant disqualification by the referee.

■ Bandages should be checked by the contest Inspector, who will stamp across the back of the hand before the gloves are secured onto the contestant's

THE JUNIOR SYSTEM OF COMPETITION FOR BOXERS AGED 6 TO 14 YEARS ENTAILS THE WEARING OF SHIN GUARDS, BODYSHIELD, GROIN GUARD, MOUTHPIECE AND 8oz GLOVES. IN COMPETITIONS IN MOST EUROPEAN COUNTRIES, JUNIOR BOUTS STRICTLY DISALLOW ANY CONTACT TO THE HEAD OR FACE.

hands. Bandages may not be worn on any other part of the body than the hands.

■ Each contestant may have three seconds of his choice, although only two seconds may enter the ring at any one time. Each second must abide by the rules of the contest. Clear water bottles, sprays or drinking bowls and buckets must be used in the corner. Only a towel, water, ice, Vaseline (petroleum jelly) and 1000-1 adrenaline are permitted in the corners. The application of liniment or boxing oil during a bout is strictly prohibited. Strictly no glucose drinks, food or any stimulant is allowed in the corner. Contestants and seconds must not consume any alcohol, drugs or stimulants before or during an event.

Conduct of bouts

■ DURATION OF CONTESTS FOR MEN

'C' CLASS	3 x 2 minutes
'B' CLASS	5 x 2 minutes
'A' CLASS	5 x 3 minutes

DURATION OF CONTESTS FOR WOMEN

'C' CLASS	3 x 2 minutes
'B' CLASS	4 x 2 minutes
'A' CLASS	5 x 2 minutes

■ Rest periods between rounds are 1 minute in duration for all bouts except the men's A-class contests, when the rest period is two minutes.

■ Immediately before the contest commences, the referee will call the two contestants to the centre of the ring to give them a final briefing.

■ The referee will declare the outcome of the contest by one of the following methods:

a) Knockout (KO)

b) Technical knockout (TKO)

c) Retired — including throwing in the towel (RET)

d) Disqualification (DISQ)

e) Referee stops contest — including injury, outclassed (RSC)

f) Decision on points (PTS)

g) No contest (NC)

h) Intentionally throwing the contest (THW)

A BOXER WEARING THE REGULATORY SAFETY EQUIPMENT REQUIRED FOR AMATEUR MUAY THAI BOUTS. THIS MAY ALSO BE EXTENDED TO INCLUDE ELBOW, KNEE AND SHIN PROTECTION.

■ All offensive Thai boxing punches, kicks, knees, elbows and striking techniques are authorized with the exception of those specified as fouls (*see* panel p89).

■ For professional Muay Thai there is a 10-point must system.

■ The principles of scoring are as follows:

i) Striking with a punch, elbow, knee or kick according to Muay Thai rules. The officials will consider the effectiveness of the technique, its strength, accuracy and how much disadvantage it causes the opponent.

j) Defensive ability to evade or block an opponent's attack.

k) In the event of equal scores at the end of a bout, the boxer who was more offensive and who fought a clean

NO WAY THROUGH! A BOXER THROWS A ROUND KICK TO THE BODY OF HIS OPPONENT WHO STOPS IT WITH A CLASSIC FOREARM AND CROSS-SHIN BLOCK.

bout, receiving no warnings for fouls, will be declared the winner.

■ Fouls may be classified at the discretion of the referee into three categories: a) warning, b) deduction of points, or c) disqualification. The referee shall base his decision on the severity of the foul, on the intent of

---

Fouls

■ Head butting.

■ Striking the groin.

■ Attacks above the shoulders with either the knee or elbow in C-class bouts only. A knee strike to the head is allowed in B-class bouts. Knee and elbow strikes to the head are allowed in all A-class Muay Thai contests.

■ Attacks to the lower back or spine with either the knee or elbow.

■ Striking the contestant when he is down (a contestant is considered knocked down when any part of his body (other than his feet) is touching the ring canvas such as a knee or glove.

■ Intentionally pushing, shoving or wrestling an opponent out of the ring (with the exception of authorized techniques).

■ Attacking on the referee's command 'yaek', also known as 'break', when both contestants have been ordered to take a step back by the referee.

■ Attacking after the bell has sounded for the end of the round.

■ Holding the ropes.

■ Purposely going down without being hit. The referee will automatically administer an eight-count (and the judges will consider this a knockdown.

■ Needless utterances or abusive language including that of the contestant's seconds.

■ Intentionally evading contact by turning one's back or going down without being hit.

■ Any shoulder, stomach or hip throw.

■ Purposeful dropping of one's mouthpiece.

■ Foot sweeps.

■ Use of the thumb to the eye.

---

the contestant committing the foul and the result of the foul. At the time of the infraction, the referee will indicate to the judges as to whether a point should be deducted from each of the judge's ballots. The referee may decide to deduct only one point, in which case he will signal to the senior judge only to deduct the point from his scorecard for that round; or he may simply issue a warning to the contestant, wherein no points will be deducted. When a warning is issued, the contestant should acknowledge the infringement by bowing his head to the referee in respect of the decision. The referee may also decide that the foul was so severe that disqualification is necessary. In this case the referee will stop the contest and declare the fouled contestant to be the winner.

■ If a referee determines that a fouled contestant needs time to recover, he may stop the contest and give the injured contestant a reasonable amount of time to recover. Should the referee (in consultation with the contest doctor) determine that the contest cannot continue, the referee shall immediately disqualify the contestant committing the foul and award the decision to the fouled contestant. However, if the referee determines that a foul was accidental, then, after allowing for recovery time, the contest will continue with no points deducted. If, after an accidental foul, the contestant cannot continue, the scores from previous rounds will be added. The declared winner will be the contestant with the most points.

■ The referee will have the power to stop the contest at any stage during the bout if he considers it too one-sided, or if either contestant is in such a condition that to continue might subject him to serious injury. No contestant will be permitted to begin any round without a mouthpiece. If it is knocked out at any time during the course of the contest, the referee shall call time-out, clean off and replace the fallen mouthpiece.

■ Should a contestant not come out of his corner when the bell sounds at the start of a round, the referee will count as though the contestant were knocked down. If the contestant has not left his corner by the end of the count, the referee will award a technical knockout to his opponent by virtue of surrender (retired).

■ When a contestant is knocked down, the referee shall order the opponent to retire to the farthest neutral corner of the ring, then immediately begin to count over the contestant who is down. A round ending before the referee reaches the count of 10 will have no bearing on the count. There is no being saved by the bell except in the final round when the count ceases and the bell is rung. If both contestants go down simultaneously, counting will continue as long as one of them is down. Should a contestant who is down rise before the count of 10 is reached, then go down immediately without being struck, the referee shall resume the count from where he left off.

■ In all bouts, the referee may at his discretion, administer a standing eight-count to a contestant who is in trouble but still standing. After completing the count the referee must determine whether the contestant is fit to continue or to declare his opponent the winner by a technical knockout.

For C- and B-class bouts, should a contestant receive a second standing-eight count in one round, the referee shall continue the count to 10 and the contestant shall be counted out. If the contestant receives a third standing eight-count at any time during the contest, the count shall continue to 10 and the contestant shall be counted out. For A-class bouts the rule is three standing-eight counts in one round or four of these in the whole contest.

■ In the event of an accident in round one that prevents one or both contestants from continuing, the bout shall be declared a 'No contest'.

■ A manager or chief second may throw the towel into the ring at any time during the contest in order to retire a contestant.

■ The decision of any bout is only final when the referee raises the hand of the winner.

Safety regulations

■ At least one registered and approved medical practitioner must be in attendance at all events as well as a paramedic unit. The doctor must sit at the immediate ringside throughout the duration of the bouts.

■ Contestants who have been counted out will be kept lying down until they have recovered. No one will touch the contestant except the referee or chief second, who will remove the mouthpiece. A doctor will then enter the ring and personally attend to the fallen contestant, issuing such instructions as deemed fit to the contestant's seconds. If a contestant has been counted out (or undergone a TKO), he shall be unavailable for fights for such time as may be deemed suitable by the doctor.

■ The administering of drugs, controlled substances, stimulants or injections to any part of a contestant's body is prohibited either before or during a contest.

Amateur Muay Thai

Although essentially amateur boxers compete to the same rules as professional Muay Thai boxers, there are several important differences:

Protective equipment

Besides the groin guard and mouthpiece, the boxers must also wear a close-fitting body shield and head guard, sometimes with the option of also wearing shin, elbow and knee protection.

Weight divisions

The weight categories for amateur bouts are:

Pinweight	not exceeding 45kg(99 lb)
Light flyweight	45.1kg—48kg(99—106 lb
Flyweight	48.1—51kg(106 lb—112 lb)
Bantamweight	51.1—54kg(112 lb—119 lb)
Featherweight	54.1—57kg(119 lb—126 lb)
Lightweight.	57.1—60kg(119 lb—132 lb)
Light welterweight	60.1—63.5kg(132 lb—139 lb)
Welterweight	63.6—67kg(139 lb—148 lb)
Light middleweight	67.1—71kg(148 lb—157 lb)
Middleweight	71.1—75kg(157 lb—165 lb)
Light heavyweight	75.1—81kg(165 lb—179 lb)
Heavyweight	81.1—91kg(179 lb—201 lb)
Super heavyweight	more than 91kg(201 lb)

Duration of bouts

These timings currently apply to both men and women competing in amateur bouts:

3 x 3 minutes with a 1-minute break

Championships: 4 x 3 minutes or 5 x 2 minutes with a 1-minute break.

Scoring

Amateur Muay Thai is judged on a 20-point must system.

Judges and referees

There must be one referee approved by IFMA and a minimum of three, but preferably five, judges to adjudicate the bouts. There must also be a chairman and three members sitting on a jury to oversee the adjudication of all amateur bouts.

Age limits

Boxers must be at least 17 years of age and not more than 37 years old to be eligible to compete in amateur Muay Thai contests. For junior or youth contests, boxers must be at least 15 years old and not more than 18 years of age.

Juniors in Muay Thai

In 1987 the British Thai Boxing Council was responsible for the inauguration of a new competition system for juniors under the age of 17 years of age. The system disallows juniors between the ages of six and 14 years to use techniques to the head or face. Junior boxers competing under these rules are required to wear body shields and shin guards as well as a groin guard, mouthpiece and 8oz boxing gloves.

The bouts in this system are fought as follows:

C-class 2 x 1.5-minute rounds

B-class 3 x 1.5-minute rounds

A-class 4 x 1.5-minute rounds

Championship bouts 5 x 1.5-minute rounds with 1-minute breaks between rounds.

When a junior boxer is 15 years old he is permitted to fight in a Muay Thai contest wearing a head guard and shin guards. The use of elbow strikes in these contests is strictly prohibited. The duration of the rounds is either 2 x 2 minutes or 3 x 2 minutes, with a 1-minute break between rounds, depending on the boxer's experience.

Junior bouts are scored on the quality and accuracy of technique to promote excellence in the art. This method also serves to train exceptionally skilled boxers for the future while, at the same time, maintaining a safe context in which young people are able to compete. The rules and regulations exist to ensure safety and fairness for all participants, while maintaining the true essence of Muay Thai, and promoting excellence in the execution of its techniques and tactics. It is crucial that all governing bodies around the world under Thailand's governance are dedicated to promoting and preserving the art of Muay Thai in its purest form.

IN EUROPE, BOXERS AGED 15 TO 17 ARE PROTECTED BY WEARING HEAD GUARDS AND SHIN PROTECTORS.

MAKING CONTACT

NATIONAL MUAY THAI ASSOCIATIONS

AMERICA

- UNITED STATES MUAY THAI ASSOCIATION (USMTA)
- 6535 Broadway, Riverdale New York NY10471.
- Tel: (+1) 212 2658888
- Fax: (+1) 212 9743209

AUSTRALIA

- AUSTRALIAN MUAY THAI ASSOCIATION (AMTA)
- 1 Edith Street, Osbourne Park, Northbridge, WA, 6003.
- Tel/Fax: (+61) 9 2275296

BELARUS

- BYELORUSSIAN NATIONAL FEDERATION OF KICKBOXING
- Room 28, Stadium Dynamo, 8 Kirova Street, Minsk.
- Tel/Fax: (+375) 172 214591

BULGARIA

- BULGARIAN MUAY THAI FEDERATION (BMTF)
- 1/29 General Gourko Street, Varna, 9002.
- Tel: (+359) 52 437248
- Fax: (+359) 52 832962

CANADA

CANADIAN MUAY THAI COUNCIL
- 10204—7 Street S.W., Calgary, Alberta.
- Tel: (+1) 403 2448424
- Fax: (+1) 403 2595849

ENGLAND

- BRITISH THAI BOXING COUNCIL & THE EUROPEAN MUAY THAI UNION
- 19 Walsden Street, Clayton, Manchester M11 4NJ.
- Tel: (+44) 161 2231495

FRANCE

- FEDERATION FRANÇAIS DE MUAY THAI
- 45 Domaine du Chateau, G1389 Chilly Mazarin.
- Tel: (+33) 1 60492249

ITALY

FEDERAZIONE ITALIANA MUAY THAI
- Via Monte Delle Gioie 3, 0019 Roma.
- Tel/Fax: (+39) 6 8171990

MALAYSIA

- MUAY THAI ASSOCIATION OF MALAYSIA (MAM)
- 135 Tingkat 1, Alor Setar, Lebuhraya Darul Aman, 05100 Alor Setar, Kedah Darul Aman.
- Tel: (+60) 4 7318129

NETHERLANDS

- NETHERLANDS KICKBOXING BOND (NKBB)
- Mercurius Street 11, 1561 PM Krommenie.
- Tel/Fax: (+31) 75 217666

REPUBLIC OF IRELAND

IRISH MUAY THAI COUNCIL
- Currenree, Corries, Bagenalstown, Co. Carlow.
- Tel: (+353) 503 27238
- E-mail: Carlow.thai@unison.ie

SWITZERLAND

- SWITZERLAND MUAY THAI ASSOCIATION
- Pfeffingerstr. 100, 4053 Basel.
- Tel: (+41) 61 361 5675
- Fax: (+41) 61 811 1023

THAILAND

SONGCHAI PROMOTIONS
- 71/23 Soi Setsiri, Samsennai, Pahayathai, Bangkok 10400.
- Tel: (+66) 2 6185314
- E-mail: songchai@muaythai.co.th

- CHANNEL 7 MUAY THAI STADIUM
- 998/1 Phaholyothin Road, Bangkok 10900.
- Tel: (+66) 2 2720235
- Fax: (+66) 2 2720227

VIETNAM

- BOXING ASSOCIATION OF HO CHI MINH CITY
- 42/36E2 Ton That Thiep Street, District 1, Ho Chi Minh City.
- Tel/Fax: (+84) 8 8216088

GLOSSARY

The translation from Thai to English is phonetic — the English form of the word given is the closest pronunciation to the Thai language.

Arjarn	master
Ayuddhaya	ancient capital of Siam
Baht	Thai currency
Bangkok	capital of Thailand
Bao Thai	Thai pads (long mitts)
Bao Tong	abdominal protector or belly pad
Bat	to block
Ching	miniature cymbals used by the Muay Thai ringside band
Chok	fight (referee's command)
Choraked Faad Hang	Crocodile Whips his Tail (spinning kick)
Daab	sword
Dadsin	a judge, to judge
Daet	kick
Daet Kaa	low kick
Daet Lam Dooah	body kick
Daet Kor	kick to the neck
Dat Doord Daet	jumping round kick
Doi Mat	punch
Dern Muay	boxing walk
Fan Sawk	cut with the elbow
Gamagan	referee
Garuda	mythical creature
Glawng Kaek	drum used by the band
Grajab	groin guard
Hook Kwaa	right-hook punch
Hook Sai	left-hook punch
Jim Tong	body punch
Jot Yang	low round kick
Kaa	polite form of address used by females
Kai Muay	boxing camp
Kang Wang	round kick

Kao	knee
Kao Drong	straight knee
Kao Loi	flying knee
Kao Noi	small knee
Kao Wang	round knee
Khun Daa Su	guard position
Koo Ek	main bout
Kraab	polite form of address used by males
Krabi Krabong	Thai weapons art
Kru	teacher
Kruang Ruang	sacred amulet worn round bicep
Kwaa	right, to the right
Kwang Liewlang	Deer Turns his Back (turning back kick)
Lok	taken from English 'to lock'
Lok Ewl	to hold or lock the body
Luk Mai	complementary tricks
Lum/Ting	to throw
Lumpini	stadium in Bangkok
Mae Mai	master tricks
Mai Sawk	wooden armshields used in Krabi Krabong
Mai See Sawk	tricks with the elbow
Mat At	uppercut
Mat Drong	straight punch
Mongkon	sacred headband
Muay Boran	old-style boxing
Muay Kaad-cheurk	fighting with bound fists
Muay Pahuyuth	the name for Muay Thai in the Ayuddhaya/early Ratanakosin period
Muay Sakhon	International boxing
Muay Thai	Thai boxing
Nak Muay	boxer
Nam Mun Muay	Thai boxing oil
Namnak	weight
Pi	Java flute used by band

GLOSSARY

Pra Jer	sacred amulet worn around bicep	Tang Kao	stab with the knee
Rajadamnern	stadium in Bangkok	Teep	front kick
Ram Muay	ritual dance	Teep Bidt	side kick
Ramakien	Thai version of Indian *Ramayana*	Ti Sawk	side-strike elbow
Ramayana	epic story of good and evil	Uppercut Kwaa	right uppercut punch
Rayong	Eastern town in Thailand	Uppercut Sai	left uppercut punch
Sai	left, to the left	Wai	to bow
Sanam Muay	boxing stadium	Wai Kru	respect-to-the-teacher ceremony
Sawadee Kraab	(for man) — hello or goodbye	Wing	to run
Sawadee Kaa	(for woman) — hello or goodbye	Wong Muay	band for boxing matches
Sawk	elbow	Yang Sarm Khum	basic footwork of Muay Thai
Sawk Klaab	reverse elbow	Yaek	break (referee's command)
Sawk Lung	circular elbow	Yok Kru	acceptance ceremony
Sawk Na	short uppercut elbow	Yud	stop (referee's command)
Sawk Tong	jumping downward strike elbow	*And finally the most important phrase at any camp*:	
Siam	former name of Thailand	Bai Ging Kao	Let's go to eat!
Tad Mala	straight uppercut elbow under chin		

PHOTOGRAPHIC CREDITS

INDEX